HULLABALOO IN OLD JEYPORE

FOR MY PARENTS

ISMAIL MERCHANT

HULLABALOO IN OLD JEYPORE

THE MAKING OF *THE DECEIVERS*

With photographs by
Mikki Ansin

Doubleday

New York   London   Toronto   Sydney   Auckland

Published by Doubleday, a division of Bantam
Doubleday Dell Publishing Group, Inc., 666
Fifth Avenue, New York, New York 10103.

Doubleday and the portrayal of an Anchor with a Dolphin
are trademarks of Doubleday, a division of Bantam
Doubleday Dell Publishing Group, Inc.

Filmset in Linotron Trump Medieval by Wyvern Typesetting Ltd, Bristol
Printed in Great Britain by Butler & Tanner Ltd, Frome and London

Library of Congress Cataloging-in-Publication Data applied for

ISBN 0–385–26059–8

CONTENTS

	INTRODUCTION	ix
CHAPTER I	INACTION	I
CHAPTER II	OBSTACLE RACE	17
CHAPTER III	BURNING ISSUES	39
CHAPTER IV	CASTING AROUND	51
CHAPTER V	KHADIM	65
CHAPTER VI	SPLIT SCREEN	79
CHAPTER VII	ARRESTING DEVELOPMENTS	91
CHAPTER VIII	FACING TIGERS	111
CHAPTER IX	IT'S A WRAP	133
CHAPTER X	HEROES AND VILLAINS	145
	CAST	153

AUTHOR'S NOTE

Jeypore is the old Anglo-Indian spelling for Jaipur, in use during the period of *The Deceivers*, when the British had to invent their own transliterations of Indian sounds. In this book I use the modern spelling 'Jaipur', although the mood of the 1820s is echoed in the title.

I overheard the following exchange between the actor Shashi Kapoor and a visiting journalist on the set of my latest film, The Deceivers.

SHASHI:	*'To be a film producer you must either be very, very rich or very, very mad.'*
JOURNALIST:	*'And which is Ismail?'*
SHASHI:	*'Mad. Completely mad.'*

Film-making is *madness. It's an obsession: an addiction worse than opium. All film-makers are mad. Independent film-producers like myself are the most extreme cases. Without the back-up support of a major studio, independent film-making is not an easy business. You put up your own money, search for finance, defer your salary, take risks, accept all the responsibilities and, after all the work you put in to make the movie, you are the last to benefit financially. You can see the madness but you still go on doing it. It's a chronic and contagious disease: as though a mad dog has bitten you. I wouldn't give it up. You don't give up.*

INTRODUCTION

I was born in Bombay, the city which has the largest and most prolific movie business in the world. My family had absolutely no connection with the film business, but there was never a time when I wanted to do anything other than make movies. As a student at St Xavier's, a Jesuit college in Bombay from which I graduated in 1958 with a BA in Arts, I put on shows and entertainments in the college. I even persuaded the principal to allow me to stage a grand show in the college quadrangle. My facility for organizing these events and for persuading famous Indian stars to appear as guests in them fuelled my determination to go to America and make films there.

Indian films that are made in India are mostly for an Indian mass audience. I grew up on those films and I enjoyed them, but those were not the films I wanted to make. Some Indian film-makers like Raj Kapoor, Mehoob Khan, Shantaram and Bimal Roy I still hold in high esteem. But the traditional Hindi films with their obligatory song-and-dance sequences and the exaggerated, emotional overacting of the performers held no interest for me as a film-maker. There were already more than enough producers turning out these films for the local market.

The imported Hollywood films, particularly those of Frank Capra, George Cukor and Alfred Hitchcock, showed me a contrast of values, and a constantly changing society. The best of those films, I realized, concentrated on story, character and atmosphere, and that's what interested me. Films that centred on universal truths had universal appeal. I thought I might be able to do something that had not been done in the cinema before: make Indian films for an international audience.

I went to America in 1958. Officially, to study for an MA in

Business Administration at New York University; unoffi-
cially, I was already planning to make my first movie.

It was in New York that I first saw the films of the great
European directors – Fellini, de Sica, Bergman, Truffaut – and
the films of Satyajit Ray, of whose work I had read in India but
had never had an opportunity to see because they were rarely
shown outside West Bengal. These films had a profound effect
on me and they were a direct influence on the kind of film I
hoped to make. This genre of cinema seemed to me more
intellectually and emotionally advanced than anything I had
seen before, and I could also recognize in it how key a figure
the director was. People talked about Hollywood films but
they *discussed* European films.

People often remark on my ability to juggle with a dozen
projects at a time. This talent appeared early, while I was still
at New York University – I also took a job at an advertising
agency, McCann Erickson, and I began work – with the help
of some friends – on my first film, *The Creation of Woman*, a
35mm theatrical short based on an Indian myth. As soon as I
graduated in 1961 I set off for Los Angeles with the completed
fourteen-minute film. It was nominated for an Academy
Award, and later that year it was shown in competition at
Cannes.

Almost the first people I got to know when I arrived in New
York were the Indian actors Madhur and Saeed Jaffrey, who
were then working and living in the city. Saeed had agreed to
narrate my film, and he told me he had narrated another film,
The Sword and the Flute, a documentary on Indian miniature
paintings, which had been made by a young American. I was
keen to meet the American film-maker because I was
intrigued that an American should choose such a specialized
subject for a film. But it was two and a half years later, on my
return to New York from Los Angeles on my way to Cannes,
that I saw *The Sword and the Flute* at the invitation of the
Indian Consul at India House, New York. I was extremely

impressed both by the film and its maker. His name was James Ivory.

I had lived in America for three years and I recognized that in Ivory there was more than just an American who knew about India. During the course of our conversation that first evening I realized that he knew about India not in a dry, academic way but with sense and understanding – something I have never encountered in an American either before or since. I realized that he was extremely intelligent and highly sensitive but what was so absolutely extraordinary was his *feeling* for India. He had just returned to New York after a year in India and Afghanistan, where he had been making his third film, *The Delhi Way*, a documentary portrait of that city, as well as a short film, which he never finished, about what lies along the Kabul River. To take a camera and shoot a film somewhere is one thing, but to understand a country and its subjects, as a historian, as an artist, as someone who can see it on so many levels, that is very rare.

Years later, when we moved on from making films in India to making films in America, England, France and Italy, I realized that this rare sensibility of entering into the spirit of a place and its people (and into its past), was a unique quality he brought to all his films.

I hope that when the history of independent cinema comes to be written Merchant Ivory will feature prominently. Although independent film-makers are not unusual now, in 1961 film-making was still dominated by the major studios and it was bold and presumptuous for a twenty-five-year-old, with one fourteen-minute documentary to his credit, to set himself up as a producer of feature films. Further, our films would be the first to throw a focus on the Indian subcontinent in a manner that was fundamental to the development of the crop of raj-inspired films that were to become so fashionable years later.

In December of 1961 Jim and I travelled to Delhi to meet

our third collaborator, Ruth Prawer Jhabvala. In Los Angeles I had read her novel *The Householder* on the recommendation of Isobelle Lennart, a well-known Hollywood screen-writer. Ruth lived then in Delhi with her husband Cyrus and their three daughters. I had never met her, though Jim had been introduced to her when he was making *The Delhi Way*.

Ruth is extremely shy and retiring. She doesn't normally talk to strangers who call her up and ask for a meeting. At first she wouldn't even agree to see us, but I persisted. Ruth finally conceded to let us buy the rights to the book, but she wanted nothing to do with the film. As we now know, Ruth not only ended up writing the screenplay for our first film but she fast became the essential third part of Merchant Ivory Productions.

Ruth has always kept a low profile as they say. As a fiction writer she can be self-contained and has complete control over her art, whereas film-making involves many people. A director's art, too, is largely within himself, but he has to accommodate others in order to fulfil it. A producer's art is much the same as a zoo-keeper's: feeding the beasts on time, finding the money for their maintenance, keeping the trouble-some ones apart, looking after their needs and cleaning up the mess. But you don't become a zoo-keeper unless you like animals, and you don't become a producer unless you like film and film people.

I have no criticism to make of Hollywood or conventional film-making. What can one say about Hollywood? Hollywood is the way that Hollywood is. The best of those films are enjoyable, and sometimes very good indeed. But think of the *price* of these films! And what other industry could carry on for so long, so wastefully, without being shut down by bankrupt and enraged shareholders? I think that early Holly-wood was a place of film-makers, of people committed to the cinema. But today it seems to be governed entirely by anonymous accountants, lawyers, agents and business managers who have commitments to personal wealth and personal glory rather than commitments to cinema. In their hands movies have become just vehicles for making (or, more often, losing) money, and Hollywood film-makers might as well be trading on Wall Street. Yet it is Hollywood that attracts the best talent available. All artists want to be successful, and Hollywood is the barometer of that success.

For Merchant Ivory it is the *film* that is important. We couldn't even begin to work on a project that didn't excite us for its own sake rather than for the financial rewards it might produce. And it is that excitement, that commitment to something good that motivates me to find the money to make the film. Money has always been a problem for us and it probably always will be because we don't make the commercial films that are immediately attractive to potential investors. Raising money is always hard because nobody likes to take risks with their money, and this is a very risky business. So each time I go looking for money I have to be so fired up with enthusiasm for the project, so certain that it is superior to anything else, that I can begin to infect potential investors with the same enthusiasm. To generate that enthusiasm there can be nothing negative about your commitment, nor can there be large, shadowy areas of doubt about the worth of the project. Somehow, we have always found one way or another to make our films (with or without money), but it has never been easy. The major studios spend someone else's money – usually a bank's. But as an independent outfit we have advantages that, to us, are much more important than easy access to money. Because we are small and self-contained we can make the films we want to make. And we can make them the way we want to make them. We don't have to compromise in order to win the approval of some committee. We don't have to consider any force other than our own wishes. The control of our films rests not with the accountants but with us, the film-makers.

Our first film, *The Householder*, was financed by ourselves. Jim used the money from an investment he had and borrowed some more from his father. I borrowed money from my father. We deferred our salaries – if we even budgeted them, which I doubt – and we operated from my home in Bombay. The film turned out well and Columbia Pictures bought the world distribution rights to a picture they would never have financed from the start. With that money we financed our next picture, *Shakespeare Wallah*. And so it went on – the money from one film was ploughed into the next. As an independent outfit we had to make one film a year to survive. Our budgets were laughable. We made complete films on what Hollywood paid one of their executives. Fortunately our overheads were minimal because we didn't have an office: we couldn't afford one. We opened our first office in New York in 1967 – five years after we started making films. Later we opened an office in Bombay. Although we had been operating from London for many years – usually from friends', like Anthony Korner's, apartments – we didn't establish an office there until 1982, when John Murray, Ruth's publisher, offered us a room in his offices on Albemarle Street. We travelled steerage – God bless standby flying. We improvised. We used our imaginations. And we made the films we wanted to make. We discovered that – very slowly – our films had an audience. So we were making the films we wanted to make and people wanted to see. Our financial rewards were negligible. Even today I still defer my salary, and when I do pay myself I plough that money straight back into the company. I have no cash wealth. But in spirit and soul I am a multi-millionaire.

Over the next twenty-five years we made twenty-six films. Some, like *Shakespeare Wallah*, are called classics. Others, like *Savages*, are thought of as cult films. I suppose we are now best known for our Indian films, like *Shakespeare Wallah* and *Heat and Dust*, and for our 'literary' films, based on novels by Henry James and E.M. Forster. The subjects of our films have been diverse and the treatments varied, but I think we have established a distinctive style. I don't think anyone who goes to the movies these days could ever mistake a Merchant Ivory film for any other. Probably because of our own backgrounds we have always been interested in and attracted to subjects which centre on the influence of one society or culture on another, or the past on the present; people who go from one place to another, their relationships, their characters: these are themes that recur.

As our films became more ambitious, so our budgets grew, but they were – and still are – a fraction of conventional film budgets. Our early years taught us that it isn't necessary to spend enormous amounts of money on a film to make it well. And you don't need to pay actors vast salaries to get them to work for you. A true actor is far more interested in the quality of a part than the size of the pay cheque. Over the years we have managed to attract very great British, American and European actors for a fraction of their usual fee. I understand that my fiscal economies have become a legend in the film industry. I can make a $3-million film look as though it cost five times that amount. I am both praised and damned for it.

American critics exercise a notorious influence on cinema and theatre managements and audiences, and their negative responses can close a film or a play overnight. In America, success is everything and no one wants to be associated with failure, so managements are embarrassingly speedy in removing anything that is remotely tainted with defeat, and audiences, therefore, are not given the chance to make up their own minds. American critics have usually appreciated the quality of our work; nevertheless, the American premieres of our films are tense times for us. Certainly we never expected the unanimous praise with which the critics greeted *A Room with a View* in 1986. It was a typically low-budget, low-key (if high-spirited) Merchant Ivory picture, in most respects no different from our other films. Two months later the film opened in London to wonderful reviews and later, all over the world, the response was the same. And audiences echoed the critics' enthusiasm. Friends began to telephone me and ask if I could help them to get tickets, because wherever the film was showing the cinemas were solidly booked or there were long lines. Who knows why *A Room with a View* was such a success? There is no formula for a successful movie, and if there were, we probably wouldn't follow it anyway.

We found we had a huge hit on our hands. For twenty-five years I had maintained that it was possible to make good films on a small budget. As I have already said, our films have had a steadily growing and loyal following. But with *A Room with a View* we extended our growing audience *and* without compromising our own standards. It had taken twenty-five years for audiences to catch up with us. *That* was the triumph of *A Room with a View*, and that was why it was so delicious to have the studios asking us, 'How did you do it? Please tell us your secret.' We had done it entirely our way.

After a success like that there is a lot of interest in what you do next. There were already several projects we were planning, to which Jim unexpectedly added another – *Maurice*, Forster's long-unpublished novel about homosexual love. At first I wasn't very keen. It was not the theme of the book that worried me – after all, we have often worked with difficult or controversial subjects. Wasn't that, finally, also the theme of *The Bostonians*? But I felt that doing one Forster immediately after another was like going backward instead of forward – which is the direction I prefer to travel. Of course the story of *Maurice* is both dramatic and interesting: it's a wonderful subject, and I knew that in Jim's hands it would be an excellent film. But at that particular time I thought we should do something completely different and perhaps come back to *Maurice* later. But Jim's determination was stronger and so we made it.

Meanwhile, I was also setting up another film in India. As

The Producers

Pierce Brosnan as William Savage (above left);
Savage transforms himself into Gopal (left); *Gopal
the thug* (above)

Helena Michell as Sarah (left)

With Shashi Kapoor at the Rambagh Palace Hotel, Jaipur (below)

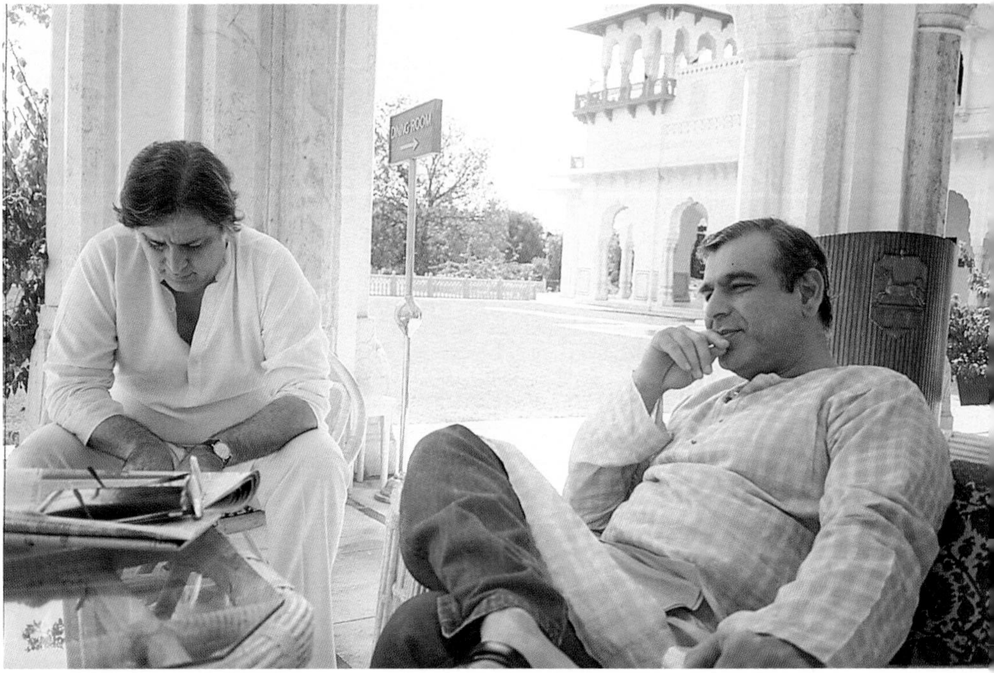

Saeed Jaffrey (right)

With Keith Michell and
Pierce Brosnan on set
(below)

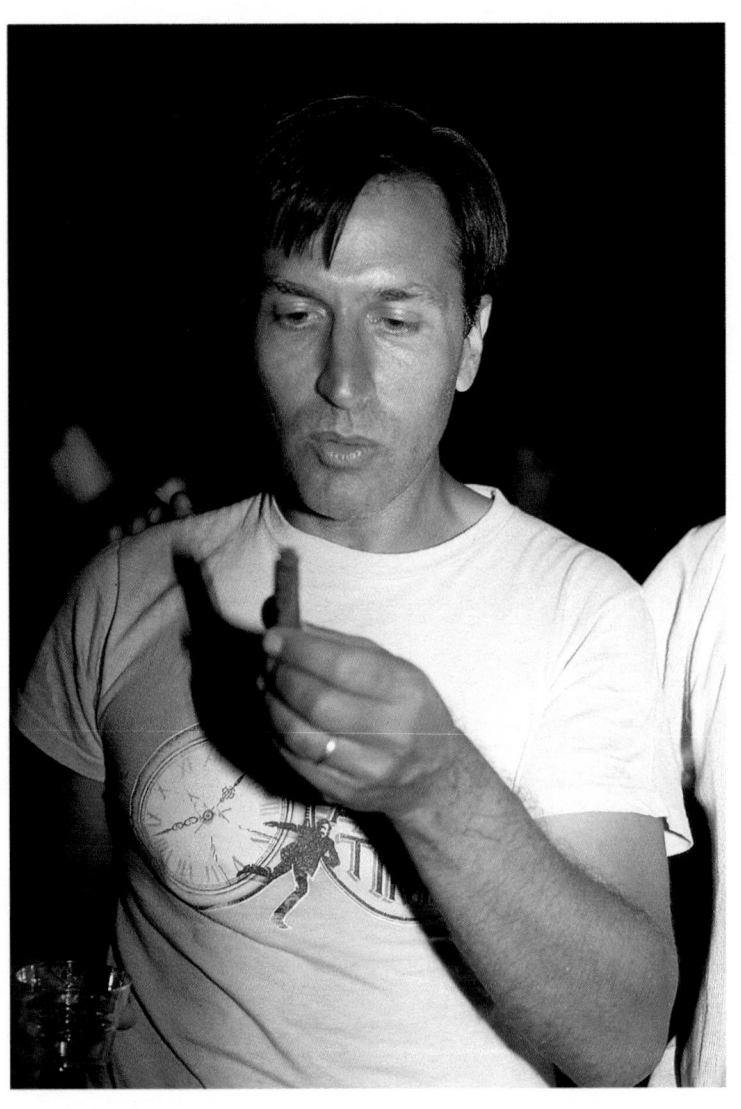

Director Nick Meyer with his ubiquitous cigar
(above)

Native beaters at the tiger hunt (above right)
and hunting the tiger (right)

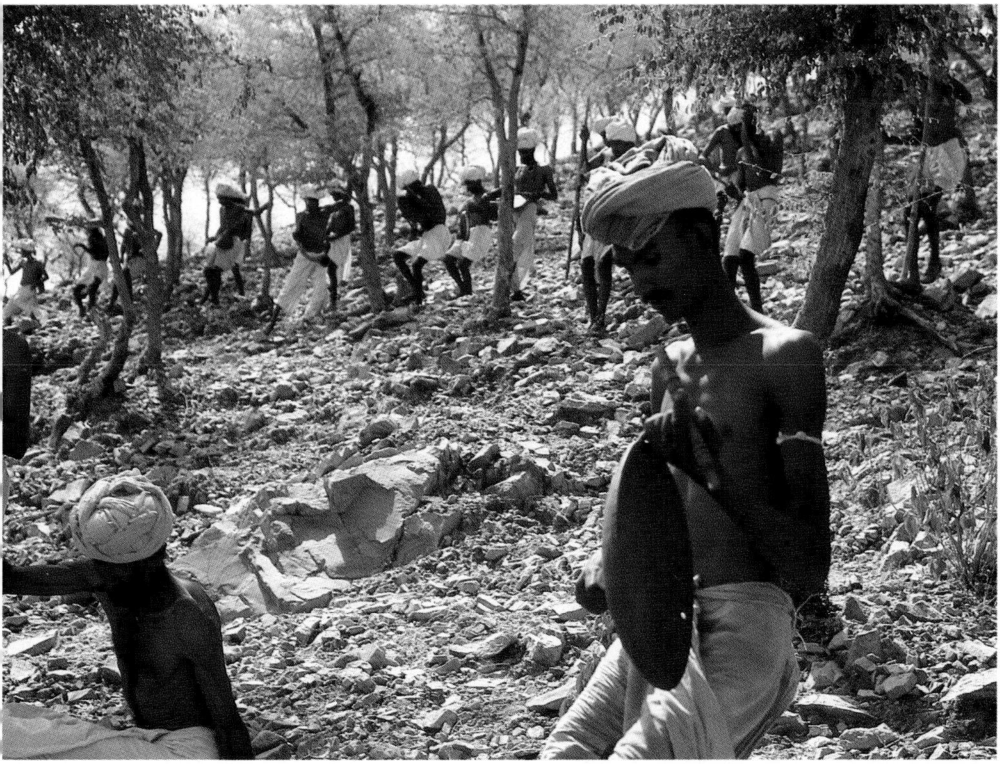

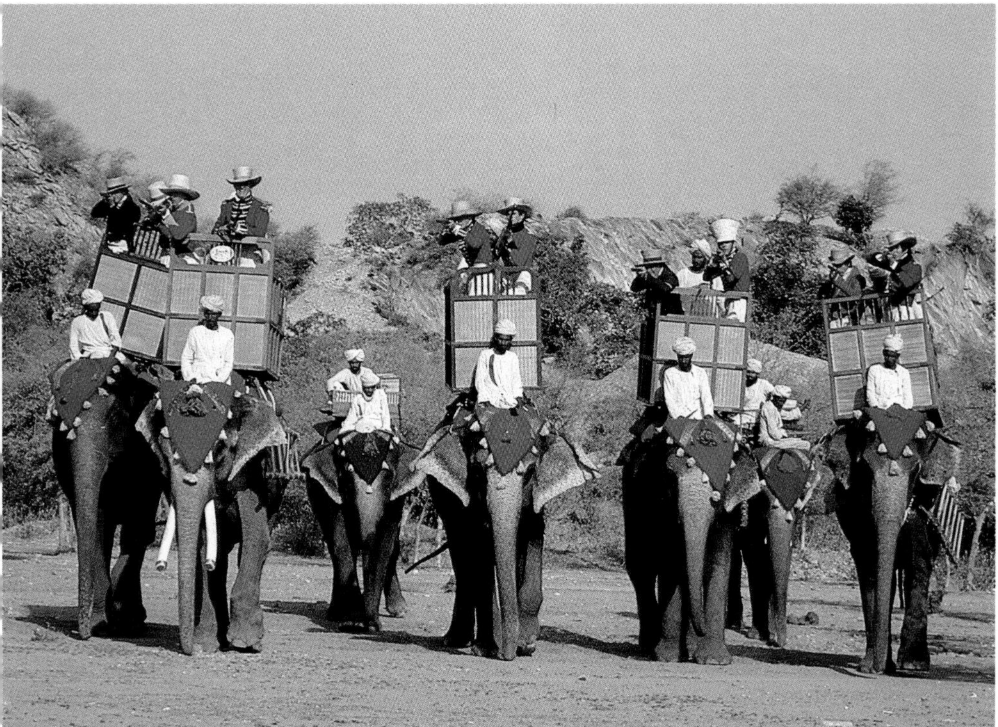

With Michael White and Keith Michell (left)

Removing a thorn from an elephant's foot (below)

far back as 1968 I had been interested in *The Perfect Murder*, the novel by Harry Keating. Jonathan Miller originally brought the project to my attention. He wanted to direct from his screenplay, which Universal Pictures had commissioned. I was ready to produce the film for him, but then someone important lost interest and the project was abandoned. But I never gave up the idea of making that film some day. Harry Keating wrote a new screenplay and now the film was to be directed by Zafar Hai.

The news that I was working with two new collaborators rather than with Ruth and Jim on this film immediately started rumours that Merchant Ivory was splitting up, especially as *Maurice* had not been scripted by Ruth. Nothing could have been further from the truth. In fact, this was a realization of a long-held desire to use new writers and directors in the same way we have always used new actors in our films. The intention had always been there but because of the way we operated in the early days it was not then a practical possibility. After all, I could hardly invite a writer and director to work on a film under the same financial arrangements I had with Ruth and Jim.

One of the greatest advantages in being an independent operation is flexibility. We don't have to seek approval from boards and committees. All the decisions rest with us and as soon as we decide on something we can get on with it immediately – or as immediately as money allows. In most cases we are not tied down to long-planned schedules, so we can manoeuvre projects to suit ourselves. Each year is unpredictable; we never really know what will materialize next or what surprises are in store for us.

And so it was at the start of 1987. *A Room with a View* was breaking box-office records, *Maurice* was in the editing room, *The Perfect Murder* was in production and Merchant Ivory found itself in the *Guinness Book of Records* as the longest-established independent film-production company in the history of movies. But there was more to come. In 1987 *A Room with a View* was nominated for nearly every major award in the industry's annual honours lists. Our films had collected awards in the past, especially at film festivals, where they generally did well – in fact, Madhur Jaffrey won our first major award when she took the Best Actress prize at the Berlin Film Festival for her performance in *Shakespeare Wallah* in 1965 – but the major awards more often eluded us. Now, suddenly, *A Room with a View* was contending for Best Picture of the year everywhere.

I don't think awards are very important in themselves. They matter far more within the industry itself than they do to the general public, who has little idea about film festivals. The idea that a heavily decorated film will attract a large audience is mostly nonsense. By the time the awards are presented the film will have already been showing for some time, and if people want to see it they are not likely to wait until some prize-giving committee indicates its approval officially. Certainly I've never been to see a film for pleasure *just* because it has won an Oscar. But to a film-maker, awards have a significance inasmuch as they focus the attention of the industry on the film and, for a time at least, you have a high profile, which is very useful professionally. Either way, if one of my films is honoured with an award, I see it as a tribute to everyone who worked on the film and I am neither so blasé nor so callous as to ignore it.

A Room with a View was nominated for eight Oscars, including Best Picture, Best Director and Best Screen Adaptation, by the movie establishment who, perhaps, have never quite known what to make of us. Less than commercial, more than 'art-house', we occupy no clearly defined cinematic niche. Our two involvements with major studios, on *The Guru* and *The Wild Party*, only served to endorse our feelings about conventional film-making and make our autonomy and precarious survival even more attractive.

xviii

CHAPTER I
INACTION

Making a film is rather like running in an obstacle race, in the sense that you have to negotiate hurdles without tripping up, but with film there is the additional handicap of having to complete the course before the time and the money run out. No matter how careful the planning or how great the vigilance, there will always be problems. For me, after all these years, most of the obstacles are familiar. I know I will encounter them and I know how to get around them. But, inevitably, each film throws up its own unfamiliar hurdles. Something will ambush you. It has happened to me many times, and I have learnt how to manoeuvre my way around even the most unprecedented obstructions.

Until *The Deceivers*, the film set has never become a battlefield. *The Wild Party* had its skirmishes, but that was different and I – like everyone else on the set – only had to do battle with Raquel Welch. On *The Deceivers* danger lay within as well as without our camp.

Since many of our films are dramatizations of books, it is shameful for me to admit that I read less than I would like. I read what is essential to my work, but beyond that I hardly have the time to read for pleasure. I don't keep as abreast of the literary world as Ruth and Jim do and I rely largely on them for their recommendations. I can, I hope, distinguish between a talented writer or a writer of merit and a writer of trash. But inevitably, I tend to view the books I read in cinematic terms. I am a slow reader and a restless one, and if I am to finish a book it must engage me immediately and completely. *The Deceivers* by John Masters was such a book.

Set in India in 1825, it is a fiction loosely based on the work of Major-General Sir William Sleeman who, as William Sleeman of the Indian Political Service, discovered, exposed and destroyed thuggee, a secret and widespread religious cult whose members ritually murdered and robbed travellers throughout India, in the name of Kali. For them she was the goddess of destruction, whom they worshipped.

In the book Savage, a young British officer in India, disguises himself as an Indian and fleetingly appears to a widow as her missing husband in order to prevent her suttee, the Indian custom of the burning of the widow on her husband's funeral pyre. In this disguise he witnesses by chance the brutal murder, robbery and burial of a group of travellers; the ritual of thuggee. He subsequently learns of the existence and practices of the thugs – Hindi for 'Deceivers' – and, horrified by what he has discovered, he decides to expose and destroy the ancient cult. But in order to do that he must penetrate their world. Once more he disguises himself as an Indian and enters a mysterious world of superstition, ritual and death. As a thug, Savage uncovers an unknown side of his personality, a mystic affinity with the blood brotherhood that is in stark contrast to his strained relationships in the English cantonments.

As soon as I finished the book I knew that I had to make a film of it. I had always wanted to make an action-thriller, and every Indian schoolboy of my generation was excited by the evil deeds of the thugs. In *The Deceivers* I saw that beneath the surface of suspense and action there was a deeper, darker core. I was fascinated by Savage's journey into a 'Heart of Darkness'; not just his journey through India with the thugs, but his journey within himself.

I thought that the very strong cross-cultural theme of the book would appeal to Ruth and Jim, but neither of them shared my enthusiasm. Jim felt that the story was too violent for him, and Ruth thought an action-thriller of this sort would be done better by a man. Both were suspicious of the main premise of the plot – that an Englishman could successfully pass himself off to a criminal band as an Indian – even though the nineteenth-century explorer and writer, Richard Burton, had done exactly that again and again, and even though Sleeman's real exploits breaking the thugs are a matter of record. I knew that if I wanted to make this film I would have to do it on my own. But this was 1968, and although we had agreed in principle to bring other collaborators into Merchant Ivory, in practice we just couldn't afford to at that stage. So the book sat on the shelf gathering dust. I knew I would come back to it.

In 1979 we released our film *The Europeans*. It did extremely well and for the first time the financial burdens on us became a little easier. I began to think again of *The Deceivers*, and I asked Jim to reread the novel, but it was clear that he would never be interested in directing this particular film. I had two options: to put the book back on the shelf to gather more dust, or to try and set up the film without him.

Jim's decision did not upset me. Ruth, Jim and I are quite different people with different temperaments. We work well together as a team, and we have been fortunate to find so many projects that appeal to us collectively, but there have been times when we have disagreed very strongly about what projects we should do – when the enthusiasm of one of us for something completely fails to rouse the others. We had already worked independently of each other from time to time and we have always accepted that we would do more independent work when the right time came.

I had been thinking about working with another director for some time; not because of any dissatisfaction with Jim, but because I wanted to have the experience of what it is like to set up a film with someone else. The impasse we had reached over *The Deceivers* seemed to present me with the right opportunity. If Jim had wanted to do *The Deceivers* then I certainly wouldn't have considered looking for anyone else, but under the circumstances I knew it would be better to find a director who would feel as enthusiastic about the project as I did.

Rank had bought the rights to the book many years back. I think there was a point about twenty-five years ago when they were seriously considering making the film, but it never happened. Major film companies often buy properties which, for one reason or another, fail to materialize as films. I started negotiating with Rank in 1981. Tony Williams, who was then in charge of production, could never understand why we wanted to make *The Deceivers*. Finally Cyril Howard, the head of Pinewood Studios, also a part of the Rank Organization, helped me to get the rights. He was obviously keen that the film be made and saw that Rank would benefit in this deal and would share in the profits. There are only a few 'men of action' working as motion picture executives, and Cyril would seem to be one of them.

As soon as I had acquired the rights in 1982, I approached Michael White, the producer, and asked him if he would be interested in putting up the money for the development of the script. I first met Michael in 1980 in New York and we had discussed the possibility of working together some day. I thought he would be interested in *The Deceivers* and I was right; he was very enthusiastic about it and wanted to be involved. He suggested we join forces for this film, and was as keen as I to get *The Deceivers* moving as quickly as possible. As a company we do not have the resources to buy properties and just sit on them, as the major studios do. I had to put the project into production quickly, and in order to do that I had to generate financing immediately. As Michael was interested, it meant that we could not only pool our resources, but that the project would have the energy of two deeply committed producers behind it.

I like Michael very much, and I think he is one of the few *real* producers in the business. He is extremely intelligent and receptive, and he has supported many new artists. When he makes a commitment to something he will see that it is fulfilled, and that sense of responsibility is rare in this business. We are both independent producers who take chances with ideas and with our own money.

I also had an enormous debt of gratitude to him. In 1984 we had just released our film *Heat and Dust*. It was our most successful movie up to that point, but halfway through the shooting part of the finance committed to the project failed to materialize and we found we were penniless. The cast and crew continued to work despite the fact that they weren't being paid, but that couldn't go on indefinitely. There was the strongest probability that we would go under. We would lose not just the film, but our whole company: the company we had spent twenty years establishing. So it was a desperate and critical time for us. The middle of shooting is certainly not the time to try and find financing. Finding the financing for a floating ship is difficult enough, but a sinking ship? I immediately began to explore every possible way to save the film and the company. It was Michael White who helped to get us out of that hole by introducing me to Sir Jacob Rothschild.

The process of setting up a film follows a set pattern. The producer either has an original script or, if it is an adaptation, he will find a writer to prepare a screenplay. Either way, the script is then sent to potential backers and investors, as well as to 'bankable' actors in the hope of obtaining a commitment. If the script generates interest and a promise of money, the producer then decides on a director. No matter how good or bad the script is, the director will invariably want to alter it to accommodate his own ideas. Sometimes the director and the writer will collaborate and rewrite the whole script. By this time the producer and the director will have begun casting. When the final script is ready, it often bears little resemblance to the first script that went out to the backers, or the subsequent drafts that the actors have seen.

7

Fortunately, I have always been spared this. I am extremely lucky in that I have always had my writer and director on the doorstep – literally: Jim, Ruth and I each have an apartment in the same building in Manhattan. Ruth and Jim generally discuss a project in detail even before Ruth begins to write the script, so she has a very clear idea of Jim's vision. They collaborate very closely during the writing, and so the script I subsequently show to investors and actors is usually quite near to the final shooting script. I knew that this time I wouldn't enjoy that advantage, but I had no idea just how complex the initial choreography between writer and director was going to be.

Michael and I approached the playwright Charles Wood to adapt the novel for us. He liked the story and he was keen to work with us. However, the screenplay he presented, though well-written and well-crafted technically, to us lacked the excitement and the tension which had made the novel so gripping. Nevertheless, on the strength of that screenplay we began to approach various potential investors and directors. We got a negative response from every single person. One of the directors we approached was Marek Kanievska, who had just made *Another Country*. Like everyone else, he wasn't keen on the screenplay, but he was willing to talk about it as a project. He read the novel, which he liked very much, and suggested making some changes to the adaptation. I felt that if he and Charles Wood were to collaborate, it might be very productive. But Wood had taken on other commitments by then and couldn't give Kanievska the time he needed. Although Kanievska was still keen to work on the film, he made it clear that he would only do so with an improved script. So we had a choice – lose Kanievska or lose the script.

Kanievska was the only director we had approached who had shown any enthusiasm at all for the project. In addition, we could see that the existing screenplay wasn't getting us anywhere with potential investors. We decided to let Wood go, and find another writer who could work with Kanievska. Kanievska suggested Michael Hirst, a young writer who had previously worked with Nicholas Roeg. Hirst prepared an outline which seemed to us to have possibilities. Neither Kanievska nor Hirst had been to India and they were unfamiliar with the culture, the landscape and the feel of the place. I thought it would be a good idea for them to take a 'recce' – an exploratory trip – in India before writing the screenplay, and I wanted to accompany them so that they could see the country with me. I felt it was important that they should experience the sights and sounds of India. I had already chosen some of the locations, which I intended showing them and which might provide some inspiration. We planned to go in March 1984 to Panna, Rewa and Khajuraho, but when the time came I found I couldn't get away because we were completing *The Bostonians* in London. Not wanting to waste any more time, I asked Aamer Hussein (who had worked with me on my documentary, *The Courtesans of Bombay*) to go with them. I knew I could trust Aamer, intelligent and well-informed, to show them everything they needed to see, and to provide the information they needed to have.

Like many people who have been to India for the first time, they were eager to communicate their impressions and experiences. Marek had been disappointed on arriving in Delhi to find wide, leafy boulevards instead of the crowded bazaars and sacred cows he had expected. But India is a land of contradictions and surprises, as he discovered when he ventured past the broad avenues into the old city and the lands beyond. The contradictions multiplied; the coexistence of beauty and decay, poverty and civility.

Michael told me of a visit he and Marek paid to one of Aamer's uncles in Delhi, and their surprise when another visitor arrived and kissed the uncle's feet. Aamer had omitted to tell them that his uncle is a Nawab and that Nawabs are sometimes still greeted in this way.

From Delhi they travelled by steam train across the desert to Rajasthan and then on to Khajuraho, where they stayed in a tree-house and fell asleep gazing out over a moonlit jungle. Michael said that he had never seen a landscape so beautiful, so old and mysterious. During the recce he had caught a bug and had been miserable and in pain and tired of the endless travelling, but as he sat in the tree top he felt calm and engulfed by beauty.

Kanievska and Hirst came back wild about India and more enthusiastic than ever about the project. We had already made some suggestions to Hirst about the screenplay and with those and his Indian trip he produced a script which we thought was very, very good.

I started sending it around to distributors and investors again, and this time people began to respond more positively. We had estimated the budget at about $4 million then, and it looked as though, with the new script, we wouldn't have too much trouble in raising it. Ernst Goldschmidt at Orion had always shown some interest in *The Deceivers*, and he immediately gave me a commitment for $750,000 against distribution rights for some international territories. It was an encouraging start.

We could now begin to think about casting. I was very keen to get Christopher Reeve for the part of Savage, the British officer. I think that because of his *Superman* image he is a very underrated actor. We had cast him, completely against that type, in our film *The Bostonians*, and everybody was amazed at how good he was in a serious dramatic part. I sent the script to him and he said that he liked the story very much and he welcomed the challenge of doing something so totally different. But before he would agree to accept the part he wanted to do a test. Of course I understood this. Halfway through the film the actor who plays Savage must transform himself from a British officer into an Indian thug. He must look convincing in both roles and he must be comfortable in both roles.

It seemed possible that we could start shooting the film at the end of 1984, and we began to work out schedules. In 1983 we had sent the script of *The Deceivers* to the Government of India for their approval. They asked for some changes, which were made, and a revised script was sent to them. We also applied for all the permissions that foreigners need in order to shoot in India. Then we had our first disappointment: Kanievska was committed to another project and wouldn't be available.

I felt the absence of Ruth and Jim more keenly than ever. Between us, we can take a decision one day and begin work the next. We can skip that whole protracted stage of finding a project, a writer, a script, a director who likes the script, an actor who likes the director, and so on. I have never taken their contribution for granted, but at this point I realized what an enormous privilege I had had for the past twenty-five years.

It was Saeed Jaffrey who suggested the director Stephen Frears to me. Saeed had just finished working on Stephen's film *My Beautiful Laundrette*, and recommended him very highly. I was open-minded, but I particularly wanted an English director because I thought it was logical to have a director who is familiar with the manners and the sensibilities of the English characters. I couldn't take it on trust that any other American director might have Jim's feeling for the English, and his ability to get on with English actors (not to speak of his insight into Indians).

Stephen read the script, but I could see he was not 100 per cent excited about it. Michael White and I agreed that the script was a good one and I wasn't prepared to start looking for another scriptwriter. But I was being unrealistic. I know perfectly well that the director's contribution to the script eventually becomes as important as the writer's. The film is the director's film: it is his vision. So if he wants to enhance a scene, or to add or to subtract, it is his right. That is how Ruth and Jim work, after all, except that they clear that hurdle very early in the course. I suppose I was becoming increasingly impatient because we had already spent a considerable amount of time, money and effort on this project and we seemed to be no nearer to the magic word, 'ACTION'.

Stephen, however, told us that he was prepared to work on the script with Michael Hirst in order to make it more to his liking. He was keen on the idea of an American playing the part of Savage. Stephen directed Christopher Reeve's screen test, which was photographed by Walter Lassally. The test worked out well and we were all happy with it. It gave us the confidence to reschedule the film for the summer of 1985. When Stephen had completed his draft of the script with Michael Hirst he sent copies to Christopher Reeve and to me. I read it that night and I disliked it. I was very upset. I'd hoped that Stephen's work on the script would improve it, but I thought that instead of making it better, he had turned it into a sort of western. I was told later by Michael Hirst that that was how Stephen saw *The Deceivers*. Christopher read the script and hated it. He also, unfortunately, had not cared for *My Beautiful Laundrette*, so we lost Christopher Reeve for the film. I conveyed my reservations to Stephen, and he finally agreed to go back to Michael Hirst's original script as everyone seemed to prefer it.

Stephen wanted me to speak to Christopher to make a final plea for him to be in *The Deceivers*. While Jim and I were in Florence doing pick-up shots for *A Room with a View*, we phoned Christopher to try and persuade him to change his mind, but he wouldn't.

Just after completion of principal photography on *A Room with a View* in July, I thought it would be a good idea to take Stephen and his designer, John Beard, to India to look at the locations and to get a feel of the place. They were excited about the possibilities and we took the opportunity of also going to Bombay to do some preliminary casting for the major

Indian parts. It began to look as though we might start shooting by the end of the year, although we still did not have our lead actor.

But the nearer we came to finalizing arrangements the further Stephen seemed to drift from the project. I realized that he was not going to make the film I wanted. He also began to develop fears about working in India; fears about the Indian technicians, fears about horses not turning up for the filming, fears about the food – he wanted British caterers to be flown in to feed the cast – etc., etc. I had made many films in India and I knew all his fears were without foundation. I had always used local caterers and none of the British cast and crew who had worked in India with us before complained. I suspected that we wouldn't have a very harmonious relationship after all, but I intended to see it through with him. I thought I might be wrong and that I should give him the benefit of the doubt. There had already been too many delays on this film and I had no intention of adding to them by falling out with the director.

By this time, we had a commitment for *The Deceivers* from Amir Malin of Cinecom for the North American distribution rights. They became an important part of financing this film. *A Room with a View* was our first collaboration and it was to make a fortune for them. Jeremy Isaacs and David Rose at Channel 4 television in London also showed enthusiasm for *The Deceivers* and committed their support, and Roger Wingate of Curzon Film Distributors was interested in being involved in the project. Orion and Cinecom were keen to have an American play the part of William Savage because of their feeling – I think a mistaken one – that an American actor is more 'accessible' to an American audience. At the beginning of 1986 Stephen came to New York to cast the part of Savage. We saw many actors, but the only one who made any impression on Stephen was Eric Roberts. Roberts is a very good actor indeed, but I was never convinced that he was right for this particular role.

I feel now that Stephen was already distancing himself from the film. The release of *My Beautiful Laundrette* had been very successful and I knew he was in demand. I also knew there was a project that particularly interested him: *Prick Up Your Ears*. I felt that if *Prick Up Your Ears* materialized, we might well lose Stephen. He had a contract with us, of course, but you cannot force people to fulfil their obligations if they don't want to.

If Stephen decided to leave the film, I wasn't prepared to accept his legacy. I hadn't yet finalized arrangements with Eric Roberts' agent, and when Stephen returned to London I decided to test one of the American actors who had impressed me: Treat Williams. Jim agreed to do the test with Treat. We shot it in Central Park, in snow and rain, Treat as Savage the officer, and a kohl-smudged Treat as Gopal, the missing weaver whom Savage impersonates. We both preferred Treat to Eric, so I began negotiating with his agent.

Back in London I learnt that Frears was becoming heavily involved with *Prick Up Your Ears*, and the likelihood was that the two films would clash. I still don't know if Stephen really did intend to make both films. In any case, *The Deceivers* seemed to be taking second place in his arrangements of his time. I received a letter from Stephen's agent, Jenne Cassarotto, telling me that the shooting of *Prick Up Your Ears* was now scheduled for July and August when Stephen could work with his friend Ian McKellen, who would only be able to make it at that time. So we could only have Stephen if we were prepared to wait until he finished *Prick Up Your Ears*. She added that this arrangement had nothing to do with our decision about Treat.

That was the first clear indication I had of where *The Deceivers* ranked in Stephen's priorities. In the end, Ian McKellen didn't make *Prick Up Your Ears*. However, the schedules by then were such that Stephen could do both films providing we could release him for post-production work on

Prick Up Your Ears. I agreed. More than anything else I wanted to get on with *The Deceivers*. Stephen, his agent and the production designer saw the Treat Williams test, which they liked, and I told Stephen I wanted Treat to have the part now that Christopher Reeve had withdrawn.

During the summer we began pre-production work on *Maurice* and I drew up a schedule for *The Deceivers*. Every time we came close to finalizing arrangements Stephen started to mention small details he said were worrying him. This time was no exception. I had noticed in the past that whenever things became difficult, Stephen would tend to hide behind his agent. Now he began doing this more than ever. His agent wrote to me to say that Stephen had not approved Richard Robbins as the composer for the film music and that we had not discussed it.

Richard has been an important member of the Merchant Ivory family since 1976, and he has composed the scores for all our films from that time. We met him in 1976 when we made a documentary film, *Sweet Sounds*, about the Mannes College of Music in New York, of which Richard was then director of the Preparatory School. He is a uniquely gifted and knowledgeable musician who understands the atmosphere each film needs and how to convey it in musical terms. I trust him as much as I trust Ruth and Jim, and it is now inconceivable to consider any other composer for our films.

I realized from my conversations with Stephen that he was still very insecure about this Indian adventure. He also seemed to feel that my involvement with *Maurice* would keep me from *The Deceivers*. That was nonsense. Stephen withdrew from the project.

And that was that. We were back exactly where we had started, except we were poorer, and had nothing to show for it.

We had to find another director, and in finding another director we might also have to find another scriptwriter and another star. Costs were beginning to escalate; something that had never happened before on one of my films.

While *Maurice* was in production, I set about looking for another director. Irving Kirschner, Arthur Penn, David Lynch, Louis Malle, Costa Gavras – we thought about and approached scores of them, and any nationality now, provided they were good, and enthusiastic about the project. Some were not available, some were not suitable and some were simply not interested. I had always wanted to work with Satyajit Ray, and I sent him the script in the hope that he would like to direct the film, but it was not to be. He felt the material was overly violent and furthermore that it lacked the interplay between characters that is his particular interest and strength.

Usually on Merchant Ivory films everything is ready for 'ACTION' without complete financing. This time the financial arrangements were completed – but I had no film and no director to shout 'ACTION'.

CHAPTER II
OBSTACLE RACE

I t was Cinecom, one of our backers and distributors, who suggested the American director Nick Meyer. I had only seen one of his films, *The Day After*, which had been made for television. He is best known as the writer of the novel *The Seven Per Cent Solution*, which he also adapted for the screen, and he wrote *Star Trek* and *Star Trek II*, also directing the latter.

Meyer has the perceptions of a writer, which is a great advantage. Seeking out his other films, I saw that he was very efficient, going directly from one scene to the next, building up plot and moving his story forward with action, rather than via characterization and atmosphere as has so often been the case with Merchant Ivory films. I had to hope that he would make enough of the darker elements under the surface of this story. There was certainly no doubt about his enthusiasm for the project. I sent both the novel and the screenplay to him and waited for his response. His enthusiasm burst through the telephone wires – he had read the novel when he was very young – it was still on his bookshelves – he had always thought it should be filmed – John Masters fascinated him – he had just heard a radio adaptation of the novel – when would we start, etc., etc? And that, of course, is exactly the kind of attitude I like.

We met in New York in January of 1987. He liked the screenplay and already had some ideas to improve it. I wondered whether Christopher Reeve might want to be involved in the film again. I arranged for Meyer to see the tests we had done on Reeve and on Treat Williams. He was not enthusiastic about either of them. He met Treat in New York, but his feeling was that it would be better to have an Englishman play the part of Savage. As he saw it, to have an

American playing the role of a British officer and then that British officer playing the role of an Indian was stretching credibility a bit far. It had to be a British actor.

We had already considered many British actors before casting the role, including Daniel Day-Lewis and Jeremy Irons. We made yet another list of British actors and Pierce Brosnan was one of them. He is best known for his American television series *Remington Steel*. Now, there is often a terrible prejudice against actors who have worked in popular television series; that they are somehow lesser actors than those who recite Shakespeare seven nights a week. I don't share that prejudice, and if Brosnan was interested in the role we would meet with him and test him and see.

Meanwhile, I had to go to Bombay to prepare for *The Perfect Murder*, another Merchant Ivory Production, which was to start shooting on 15 March 1987.

While I was in Los Angeles just before the Oscars a meeting was arranged between Pierce, Nick Meyer and myself in the Polo Lounge at the Beverly Hills Hotel. Both Nick and I liked Pierce very much and decided he would be the perfect Savage. Pierce had known about the film, and had read the script and welcomed the opportunity to play a challenging role. But it almost didn't work out that way. Nick sometimes has a very abrupt, even an explosive manner. After we had all introduced ourselves, Nick suddenly exclaimed, as if he had received a big shock, 'Oh my God, he's got *blue* eyes! What are we going to do?' I saw the problem immediately: any actor who was to transform himself from Anglo-Saxon to Indian – in a film set in the 1820s – would clearly have to start with brown eyes. Nick went on: 'I guess he'll just have to wear contact lenses. My God, blue eyes! You have blue eyes!' Pierce maintained a cool dignity but said that he couldn't possibly wear contact lenses because he had a phobia about putting anything in his eyes. I tried to change the topic by speaking about all the beautiful

Indian locations, and we started to discuss the character of William Savage and how it might be played. We all became more relaxed, and Pierce was even prepared to listen to talk of contact lenses. Nick suggested a special optician in Los Angeles to manufacture the brown lenses we needed, and he left at that point to go back to his office at Paramount Studios. Pierce and I went on drinking Irish coffee and talking about the film.

Nick suggested Ken Adam as the designer of the film. Adam is one of the most distinguished stage and film designers in the business. He has designed stunning opera sets, many of the Bond films, and he won an Oscar for *Barry Lyndon*. His reputation is for working on big-budget movies. Nevertheless, I very much wanted to work with him. He was also in Los Angeles, so we arranged to meet. I have never had very good relationships with art directors or production designers. I have always regarded them as a necessary evil, and my manner sooner or later conveys this idea to them, which is unfortunate. I've always felt they are wasting the production's money, even when I know perfectly well that they aren't and I am delighted with what they come up with. I knew that for *The Deceivers* we would have to have a designer with flair and a knowledge of the period, who could bring to the film the atmosphere it needed, and be able to function in a country he did not know and with artisans he had not trained.

Now, having worked with Ken Adam, I admire him more than ever both as an artist and as a person. He had never been to India before, which surprised me. Before we went on the recce there, he spent weeks and weeks in concentrated research. His feeling for his work was on a completely different plane to nearly all the other art directors I have worked with. On the recce he absorbed everything and he seemed to understand instinctively what the film required. I was amazed at how his final concepts reflected, and were so in tune with, the country and its textures and moods. His work absorbed him completely yet, in his very few spare moments, he was wonderful company. He never once complained: not about the inevitable inadequacies, not about the enormous workload, not about our limited budget or the heat and the hardships. And never did he utter the word 'impossible'. We were very lucky to have him, as well as his Italian wife Letizia, who acted as his assistant.

I had imagined the greatest obstacle between Ken and us would be the shortage of money, but that wasn't the case at all. I now know why. Much later, he said that when I told him what his budget would be and what the demands of the film were, he thought it was so preposterously unrealistic that one of the reasons he wanted to do the film was that he was curious to see if it *could* be done. He saw it as a challenge – and in the event he rose to it magnificently. Paradoxically, it was Michael White and Film Finances (who were guaranteeing the film) who were not keen on him. They thought such a high-profile production designer – one who had millions at his disposal on the Bond pictures – would be out of our financial league. I told them that there are sometimes pleasant surprises in our business and that we should get Ken before he took on another assignment.

While we were in Los Angeles, I took Nick and Ken to the Los Angeles County Museum to see the fine collection of Indian miniature paintings there. I had already shown them the photographs we took on the previous recce, but of course it was necessary to go to India once again with my new director, production designer and co-producer, Tim Van Rellim, and we set out in July – not an easy or pleasant assignment for people who have never been to India in the summer's heat.

One of the conditions of Meyer's contract was his approval of the cameraman and some other key personnel. I had always wanted Walter Lassally to shoot this picture, and I now hoped Nick would agree. Walter is a member of the Merchant Ivory family and a very good friend. I have a great respect for him.

He likes making films for the sake of film. Like us, he is motivated by interesting work.

We had met in 1970. Subrata Mitra, who had photographed most of our films until then, had invited Walter to a screening in London of our latest film, *Bombay Talkie*, which Mitra had shot in India. I knew him as the cinematographer of such superbly shot films as *Tom Jones* and *Zorba the Greek*, for which he won an Oscar. We were at that time setting up our documentary, *Adventures of a Brown Man in Search of Civilization*, about the Indian writer Nirad Chaudhuri, and I suggested to Jim that we should get Walter to shoot it. Jim said 'Don't be ridiculous. You can't ask such a renowned cameraman to work on such a small film. Anyway, he wouldn't be interested in working with *us*.' But I asked him anyway and he said yes. And that's one of the things I like about Walter. He doesn't care about the size of the film. He's only interested in the *kind* of film. Immediately after the Chaudhuri film, we asked him to photograph *Savages* for us, and that is considered to be one of his most beautifully lit films. Since then he has photographed many of our films. One of his most admirable qualities, aside from his professional skills, is his ability to communicate and get on with local technicians of any nationality. I have found so often that British and American technicians believe that their technical achievements are greatly superior to those of foreigners. Walter has none of those feelings. He treats everyone with equal respect – the respect of one talented man for another.

Fortunately Nick got on well with Walter and approved him as cameraman. This was a great advantage because not only had Walter worked in India many times, and so knew the country and the people and the difficulties to be found there, but he had recently shot *The Perfect Murder* for us and I knew he could call on those technicians with whom he had already established a good working relationship.

Nick also approved the team of Jenny Beaven and John

Bright to design the costumes. They, together with Gianni
Quaranta and Brian Ackland Snow, the production-designer
team, had won Oscars for *A Room with a View*. Jenny, too, is
part of our extended family. Like Walter, she builds up a
wonderful rapport with the local people working in her department. She is not only very talented, she is also absolutely
indefatigable and, most important of all, she understands the
way we work. Jenny came into our lives during the making of
Hullabaloo over Georgie and Bonnie's Pictures, when she
came out to India with Peggy Ashcroft. Jenny was already well-
established as a costume designer in the theatre and she was
enormously useful to us in that film, which was her first. (She
also, reluctantly, appeared in it as the Scottish governess.)

Meanwhile, apart from the selection of a crew, there were
other serious problems to consider. The budget for the film
had been done two years earlier – and two years is a long time
in this business. The original budget of $4 million was now
closer to $6 million. Costs rise all the time, and if we didn't
start the film soon, we would have to start thinking of even
more money. A budget of $6 million is not particularly great,
but it was twice the size of anything we had done before. We
had brought in both *A Room with a View* and *Maurice* at $3
million each and had felt profligate. I knew that no one else
could make *The Deceivers* for as little as $6 million, and it
was only my knowledge of India and my contacts there that
would make it possible at that figure, but I still had the problem of finding the extra money. I approached Cinecom, Channel 4 and Orion to increase their investment to accommodate
the shortfall. Cinecom and Channel 4 agreed to increase their
original investment, but before Orion could increase their
investment they had to wait and see how the film would turn
out. I went to Roger Wingate of Curzon Film Distributors to
put up more money for the UK distribution. Roger Wingate
had put money into several of our films in the past, and he has
done well with them, not only on the initial investment, but

also by releasing our films in his London cinemas, where they've been particularly profitable for him. And so began the following exchange:

From: Ismail Merchant
To: Roger Wingate
22 May 1987

Dear Roger,
. . . The budget of the film has increased to $6·2 million. All the parties, including Channel 4, have been asked to increase their participation by 25 per cent. Do you think Curzon would consider $350,000 advance guarantee for the Theatrical/Non-Theatrical rights?

This letter was sent off before I noticed a critical error.

From: Ismail Merchant
To: Roger Wingate
26 May 1987

Dear Roger,
Further to my letter dated 22 May, the amount of $350,000 should be in sterling not in dollars. We need £350,000 towards *The Deceivers*.

From: Roger Wingate
To: Ismail Merchant
28 May 1987

Dear Ismail,
Taken together, your letters of 22 and 26 May are an Ismail classic. Perhaps I should have replied with an instant 'yes' to the first one!

How I wished he had. He went on to say that it had been Frears' involvement in the film that had made the proposition attractive to him initially, and he was not prepared to go ahead with Nick Meyer, who he thought was largely an unknown quantity in Britain as a director.

In the end, Roger Wingate was prepared to put up $450,000 for 25 per cent of the profits! This I could not agree to. I had worked for seven years to get this film going and even *I* would not be seeing that kind of a return. So now I had a film which was ready to go into pre-production but, not untypically, with incomplete finance. We still had to come up with a shortfall of $650,000.

Now production offices were being set up and all the key elements were being assembled. We had organized a test for Pierce, the results of which revealed that he was going to be very, very good. Orion and Cinecom were very enthusiastic about our choice of Pierce Brosnan, which seemed to satisfy everyone's needs, as he is very well-known in America.

This test also revealed that we had a problem. The first indication I had was a long memorandum from Tim Van Rel-lim, after Pierce's test shoot, in which he complained at length about the camera equipment, which we owned, found fault with everything, laid down the law about how produc-tion money should be spent and ended, finally, by telling me how he was going to make *my* picture. Fundamentally I felt he didn't understand my way of making films, and didn't use my extensive experience of producing high-quality films on a low budget. Tim Van Rellim had been hired by me as, to all intents and purposes, a line producer to work at my side. But at his request we gave him the more impressive title of co-producer, although this didn't alter his function. However, he acted at times as if the title gave him a producer's power without any attendant worries. He had been brought into the film at the same time as Stephen Frears. I knew him briefly from *A Room with a View*, for which he had done a budget breakdown for us before we began, but he didn't work on the film. I knew that his background was in accountancy and that was useful. He had worked for Michael White and for Stephen

Frears before and I had heard nothing from them to suggest just how different our approaches would be.

At the time his memorandum simply struck me as being impertinent and pompous. Obviously we wanted to use our own camera equipment to save money. But it isn't the responsibility of the people who store our equipment to check its condition. It is the camera assistant's responsibility to make sure that all the components are available and in working order, and to do this long enough in advance so any problems can be solved before arriving on location. It was either the line producer's or production manager's responsibility to see that the camera assistant had done this.

I was aware by this time that Tim had started politicizing everything and seemed to be trying to create rival camps. Everyone who has ever worked on a Merchant Ivory picture has always commented on the family atmosphere on the set, and that is something I actively try to foster. I think people are happier and work better when everyone is united and gets along. Considering that Tim was working on our film of his own volition, and that he was getting a very generous pay packet from us each week, I couldn't understand his attitude to Merchant Ivory which began at this time. For example, I heard from Rita Mangat, who always makes our travel arrangements and gets the best possible deals with Air India for us, that he wanted to use another travel agency with a twenty-four-hour operation. He told her that *The Deceivers* was not a Merchant Ivory film and that she would not be able to handle such a huge production. He was trying to assume the role of producer and trying to put me in the role of financier. He even said that because Merchant Ivory had never made an action-thriller before, we had no idea how to go about it and that if he didn't manage the whole show and get the right production people we would be in a mess. I heard similar stories from Fahad Samar, the son of a very dear friend of mine, who at his request was on set keeping a diary of the filming to use as the basis for a college report.

As far as I am concerned, each film has its own demands whether it is a film with five characters or 5,000 characters. Each film has its own production problems. Certainly Merchant Ivory had never done an action-thriller before, but that did not mean we were not capable of doing one. If I had thought for one moment that I couldn't do it, I wouldn't have begun. We retained Rita Mangat.

Before leaving for the recce to India at the end of July, I had given Nick, Ken and Tim a list of the locations that I thought were possible and also some suggestions coming out of the earlier recces done by Frears and by Kanievska. I joined them when they were in Khajuraho, a very remote place known primarily for its temples covered with erotic sculpture. I introduced them to Lokendra Singh, the Prince of Panna, and his wife, who were enormously helpful to us and offered us their assistance when we came to shoot there later on. I then went to Agra and from there to Jaipur. We had not intended to use Jaipur as a location for the film, and were planning instead to use Jodhpur. But it was obvious at once that Jaipur had many possibilities. There was a huge variety of useful shooting areas within and without the city at no more than forty-five-minutes' drive, and the city itself had excellent hotels and other facilities which would help the production to function efficiently. I had asked Deepak Nayar, who had been our production controller on *The Perfect Murder*, to be the Indian production manager on *The Deceivers*. He was accompanying us and had made preliminary arrangements for this recce.

Deepak introduced us to Bonnie Singh, with whom he had worked on *The Far Pavilions*. Obviously, the purpose of this introduction was to find Singh a job on the film. We met briefly in the lobby of the Rambagh Palace Hotel, where we were staying. It was a very informal meeting and I didn't have time to talk to Singh for very long. He seemed competent and since Deepak had worked with him, and I trusted Deepak, I expected him to be good. When I returned to Bombay, I drew up a list of some of the people we had seen on the locales whom we might employ. I included Singh's name on the list.

The film world is much smaller than people imagine. I think the old adage about one person sneezing and everybody catching a cold is applicable. I soon discovered that Bonnie Singh's reputation was somewhat unsettling. I had heard various stories about him that made me cautious of employing him. I contacted Deepak and told him I didn't want Singh on the film under any circumstances. Singh had apparently worked with Deepak for two days on the recce, so we paid him for his two days and as far as we were concerned that was the end of it. Yet I had a suspicion that he might still cause trouble for us.

The hiring of technicians and production people is usually a function I perform myself. I know how important it is to get people who are not only good but who can work well together. On a film, especially one shot on location, you are working and living with the same people for months and, although it would be unrealistic to expect everyone to be great friends, careful selection goes a long way towards ensuring that the atmosphere is congenial and there are no major clashes of temperament. On this occasion, however, because I had to go to America to arrange the opening of *Maurice*, I had to leave Tim Van Rellim to organize putting much of the English crew together. Tim filled key positions with people who I thought were not likely to create the family atmosphere I like. When he later threatened to leave the picture, I would have given my blessing if, in particular, three people, hired by Tim, had gone with him: the production supervisor Tony Waye, the accountant Alex Matcham and the production coordinator Dena Vincent, whose ideas, I felt, did not correspond to our economical way of making films.

Tim had hired Tony Waye in July. Although at that time it seemed that the film was finally going ahead, we still weren't absolutely certain, and I thought it was pointless to put people on the payroll and make commitments to them at that stage.

Things fall into place as you move along – production takes on a life of its own. However, before our departure for India we had made a commitment to Tony Waye because Tim had such unnecessary anxieties about the production.

We had a six-week pre-production schedule, with shooting to begin on 21 September. The weather in India would still be uncomfortably hot, and the pre-production time was too short, but I had waited too long to make this film to consider postponing it even by a day. As for the pre-production time, it is never enough. It is wise to have a decent pre-production period, but still it always turns out to be too short. More time would have been useful, but we simply didn't have it. We had equally tight schedules on *Maurice* and *A Room with a View* (and on every film we ever made) and we had managed to accomplish everything we needed within those schedules. But Tim was worried, and he would reply that *The Deceivers* was a far bigger movie.

Just before the unit was due to leave for India at the end of August, Nick and Tim came to see me. Nick hinted at replacing Walter Lassally, our cameraman. I knew that they had got on with each other when they first met, and I asked Nick whether anything had happened since. He suggested that Walter did not seem amenable to new ideas and was not willing to use the new stock and the new lenses that we had. Instead of being angry, as I should have been, I roared with laughter. I have known Walter too long and worked with him too closely to accept that. Walter is the last person in the world not to use new ideas – he is easily the most innovative and versatile cameraman I know. I told Nick that if Walter wasn't doing the picture then neither was anyone else – there would be no picture. The message got through.

During the recce with Nick and Ken I had sensed that Tim was trying to convince them that it was he who was responsible for this production and only *he* who could deliver the goods. He also took advantage of their insecurities; inse-

*Tariq Yunus as Feringea and Shanmukha Srinivas
as Hira Lal, his adopted son*

Ken and Letizia Adam

Tim van Rellim appears briefly as the Reverend
Matthias in the wedding scene

With James Ivory at Khajuraho (above)

Walter Lassally (below)

Michael White in costume for the ball scene

While off-duty, Helena Michell visits her father Keith Michell on set (left)

With Saeed Jaffrey on set (above right) *and Saeed as Hussein* (below right)

In the lunch tent (below)

Tariq Yunus has his turban tied (left) and Shashi Kapoor is gift-wrapped by the wardrobe department

curities about working in India, where neither Nick nor Ken had been before, about our economical methods of working and so on. At this time he began creating a myth that Merchant Ivory were distrusted because we had a bad reputation for paying people. In fact, he once said that to me. The only reply I could make was to ask him why, if that were so, the same people, both actors and technicians, have returned to work with us again and again over the years. Nick is rather impressionable and came under the influence of Tim's views. Ken, on the other hand, has a stronger character and a broader experience of the film world, so he was more resistant to Tim's influence.

Greater than all the other pre-production headaches, I still hadn't found the extra money we needed to finance the picture totally. Fortunately, because we have a good relationship with Credit Lyonnais, the French bank, we could continue to work on the production while I tried to find another investor to make up the shortfall. Credit Lyonnais customarily puts up the costs for production and acts as financiers against distribution contracts that are often payable on delivery of the finished picture. The bank also looks for a collateral in case anything goes wrong with the distribution contracts. I had no alternative but to offer as collateral the most valuable property that I had. I assigned to them the profits of *A Room with a View*. At the eleventh hour I raised the $650,000 shortfall from the Falkhan Group, a new, young and energetic company that plans joint ventures with the United States and European investors in high-quality entertainment.

The time it took to finalize the deal with Falkhan and then with Credit Lyonnais meant there would be a delay before we could begin transferring our money to Jaipur. Tim started to panic, and panic is not something I like. I arranged for my brother-in-law, Wahid Chowhan, a successful businessman in Bombay, who had just produced *The Perfect Murder*, to advance money to Tim as a favour to me until the money arrived from London. I also sent a message to Tim telling him how much I would appreciate the *calm* handling of financial and overall production problems. Unintentionally, that telex was the opening salvo in what became a telex war between London and Bombay. Tim immediately fired a telex back lecturing me about our finances, despite the fact that the money had now been transferred to Bombay. He added that it was only his calm endeavours that had kept everyone together and that most had wanted 'to up stumps and go home'. There was only one possible reply to that.

TELEX
From: Ismail Merchant
To: Tim Van Rellim
27 August 1987

Thank you for your telex. People who want to up stumps and go home. Please send them home before I arrive in India.
I will not tolerate any nonsense.

That, apparently, merited a double-barrelled reply. First a telex to let me know that he would not tolerate any nonsense either, and threatening that if he were to leave, Nick Meyer, Ken Adam and Tony Waye would leave with him. This was rapidly followed by a further telex to me and Michael White, insolently accusing *us* of not being aware of the complexities of the film, adding, 'I must advise you that I can no longer accept responsibility for actions undertaken without my agreement.' Whether or not it was wishful thinking, both Michael and I understood this to imply that if we weren't prepared to meet his demands he would resign. We sent a telex back accepting his suggestion of withdrawal, while allowing the others to decide individually what they wished to do. Tim immediately sent a telex informing us that not only had he not resigned, but he had no intention of resigning.

I had been very angry with the first telex, and my anger increased each time the telex machine spat out another of his impertinent and high-handed messages. 'Just who the hell is he?' I asked myself. Michael White felt the same way and wanted to get rid of him too. I despise weepy people who are always complaining. He wanted to be known as co-producer, but it seemed to me he wasn't functioning as a straight-forward line producer without continually firing off telexes to us in London, which is all we were asking of him. A line producer is there to hold the fort, not to worry about the foundations, which is for the producer. If you are a producer you must behave like one; along with the power and the prestige you must take the burdens and the responsibilities, both for the production and for the financing.

If I had been in India, my immediate reaction would have been to put him on the next plane for London. Both Michael and I were furious that he had presumed to tell us how to make *our* film. Nick Meyer telephoned me from India and asked, before I did anything final or drastic, that I wait until I came to India to discuss it with them. Gilda Smith from Film Finances also called and suggested I should go to India and sort things out as soon as possible.

I drew up a memorandum of things that needed to be said in India.

MERCHANT IVORY PRODUCTIONS

Tony Waye and others telling everyone that this is not an MIP film.

Merchant Ivory is the one who hires everyone – Nick Meyer, Ken Adam, etc. – and I do not wish to hear any more of their production philosophy.

FINANCE/PEOPLE

The production finance will be controlled by Merchant Ivory and no one else.

Who is hired and fired is solely the decision of Merchant Ivory. Before any decision is made, Merchant Ivory is to be consulted. The hiring of the entire India crew has been and will continue to be done by Merchant Ivory, including actors.

We will not have any more telexes threatening resignations.

From now on this is a Merchant Ivory Production.

When I arrived in Bombay on 1 September, Tim telephoned Merchant Ivory's office from the Taj Mahal Hotel where he was staying, and asked Shahnaz, my secretary, if I could meet them there. Shahnaz told him that the lobby of a hotel was not the place for such a discussion, and suggested they come to my office instead. When Tim and Nick arrived they were subdued and apologetic. They appeared to want a reconciliation and to continue to work on the film. I made it clear that as long as they understood that the control of the film began and ended with Michael and me, and that I was not prepared to compromise the film over what I perceived as a power struggle, I would accept their apology. And there was something else that was felt, if not actually said: although Jim had not wanted to direct *The Deceivers*, when he saw the problems I was facing he promised that if anything went wrong and I needed his support and help, he would be there and that he would, if necessary, direct the film. His readiness to come to India (in fact, he was most unready as he was enjoying himself in Venice, but I knew I could always count on him) was presumably not lost on Nick.

The next obstacle I would have to face, however, was infinitely more sinister and dangerous. Tim had brought with him from Jaipur a press clipping from *The Times of India*, dated 29 August 1987.

It said that Basant Vyas, the general secretary of the Council for Social, Political and Economic Studies, had written to the Chief Minister of Rajasthan, Harideo Joshi, to demand that the shooting of *The Deceivers* be stopped because it presented a distorted picture of Indian mythology and culture. A delegation of the council had also met the Minister of the Environment, Mr Sheesh Ram Ola, and the Minister of Culture, Mrs Kamla Beniwal, urging them to prevent the unit from using the forest areas in the state for filming.

This news surprised but did not particularly disturb me. However, on 2 September a news item in *The Times of India* stated that another group, the Jaipur Sarbojanian Durga Puja Committee, were also claiming that *The Deceivers* showed the traditional culture and heritage of India in a poor light. Mr S. N. Das, the president of the committee, said that the film was critical of traditional values and depicted the goddess Kali as an evil spirit.

My only reaction to these reports was that they were nonsense. The Government of India had approved the script and granted us permission to shoot the film. I had no idea who these pressure groups were or what they were ultimately trying to do, and I had too much on my mind to worry about them. Between 3 and 13 September I commuted between Jaipur, Delhi and Bombay, where I had a series of meetings with the Ministry of Information and Broadcasting, the Defence Ministry, Indian Customs and various other ministries to finalize arrangements for the shooting.

I left India on 13 September. The opening of *Maurice* in New York was on the 17th, and on the 21st I had to be in Washington DC for the twenty-fifth-anniversary tribute to Merchant Ivory from the American Film Institute. I had known that the start of shooting in India would clash with the American opening of *Maurice* and the retrospective exhibition of our films in Washington. It would be the only time I had missed the first day of shooting on one of our films, but I had accepted the invitation from Washington a year earlier and as we were the guests of honour and, indeed, the reason for the event, I could not consider cancelling that arrangement. An assembly of our actors and long-time collaborators was to be a part of this tribute, with people flying in from all over the world.

As soon as I arrived in New York I began getting frantic telephone calls from Jaipur. The pressure to ban our picture was mounting, and letters had been written to the Ministry of Information and Broadcasting by Basant Vyas, who had initiated the campaign, and Sunaina Mishra, a social worker. During one of the telephone conversations I heard that it had been reported in the press that Vyas and Mishra had managed to get the support of the Minister of Culture in Rajasthan, Kamla Beniwal, and the Collector of Jaipur. Over the next week the reports that were coming from Jaipur were more and more disturbing. The first day of shooting had been disrupted because the Collector insisted that the local authorities had not granted permission.*

The Collector's stand about 'local authorities' was nonsense. We had the permission from the Government of India and didn't need local authorities to give a ruling over and above the Government's permission to us. But the shooting schedule had to be quickly changed to another scene which was to be shot on private property over which the local authorities had no jurisdiction, and I conveyed this information to Tim from New York.

Basant Vyas, meanwhile, offered a deal, in which he promised to stop all this harassment. I wanted nothing to do with this. Even more, I wanted nothing to do with him. Everything I had done has been legal and above board. The Central Government of India had approved the script and the making of the film. I had not hired Bonnie Singh in order to

* The term 'Collector' comes from the old Indian Civil Service, which administered India under the British. The Collectors were originally responsible for collecting the taxes from each region. Now they are responsible for law and order in the cities. Each city has a Collector, and the police are under his jurisdiction.

avoid such problems, and Vyas wasn't even working on the film.

Tim had called on the Chief Minister of Rajasthan and threatened to commit public suicide if the local government would not grant permission to shoot the film, and he undertook a personal guarantee to face arrest if anything offensive was shot. Obviously Tim had no intention of committing suicide, either publicly or in private. Although I felt his actions may often have been unfortunate I had no doubt of his commitment to the film. Tim also met with the Secretary of the Ministry of Culture, Govindji Mishra, and he was finally given temporary permission to shoot for three days. I sympathized that in my absence Tim, a foreigner, had to deal with the officials. I asked Wahid Chowhan, my brother-in-law and a native of Rajasthan, to do as much as he could to help. Tim got the production going at a time when we risked losing time, money and morale, and that was an enormous help. Without his tremendous initiative at this stage, filming might have come to a standstill. Tim gave the local government a sworn statement taking full responsibility should they film anything derogatory or offensive. Yet for all that the crew were still being stoned by local demonstrators and there were constant attempts to sabotage the equipment.

I flew from New York to Washington on the 21st and met with Shashi Kapoor, who had also been invited to the celebrations. The Indian Ambassador to Washington, His Excellency Pratap Kishen Kaul, also attended the celebrations at the American Film Institute, and he invited Shashi and myself to lunch at his residence. This luncheon was a good opportunity to bring the developments in Jaipur to the Ambassador's attention and to seek his help. I told Kaul about the problems we were having in Jaipur and he was very sympathetic. Like everyone else, he thought the whole uproar quite ridiculous and he offered to speak to Girish Mehra, Secretary of the Ministry of Information and Broadcasting, Balkishan Zutsie,

Joint Secretary of the Ministry of Information and Broadcasting and Mr S.K. Misra, Secretary of the Ministry of Tourism.
Kaul said he would do everything he could to help. He was an
influential man, and I knew his efforts would have positive
results.

Planning strategy in far-off Washington was all very well,
but I felt the need to be in India very keenly.

CHAPTER III
BURNING ISSUES

I took the direct Air India flight to Delhi; my mind was full of the people I would have to see who might be able to help resolve the controversy over our film. I arrived in Delhi on 23 September and immediately arranged to meet with Girish Mehra, who had already been briefed over the telephone by Ambassador Kaul in Washington. Mr Mehra was expecting my arrival and wanted to reassure me of the support of the ministry. He promised that he would do everything in his power to see that the shooting of our film would not be disrupted, and advised me to continue shooting unless I heard to the contrary from his ministry. Mr Mehra said he would write a letter to the Chief Secretary of Rajasthan, Mr Mathur, reiterating the support of the Ministry of Information and Broadcasting, and he gave it to me to take personally to Mr Mathur.

The Ministry of Information and Broadcasting is very important; it controls cinema, radio, television, the press and all news media. It is through this ministry that the Government's thoughts and ideas are communicated to millions and millions of people in India and abroad, and to a large extent it influences what is happening in cinema, theatre and the arts. It is also responsible for granting permission to foreign film-production companies to shoot their films in India. Scripts have to be submitted for examination by the ministry, which then has the power either to grant permission for the film to be made, reject the script or, alternatively, recommend the modification of the script as per the ministry's views. If permission is granted, a liaison officer is appointed by the ministry to be on set throughout the shooting, to make sure there is no deviation from the approved script.

In 1968 the French director Louis Malle came to India to

make a series of documentaries called *Phantom India*. These films were Malle's own impressions of India and, although there was no script, the Government gave permission for the films to be made and Malle was given enormous help by both the Ministry of Information and Broadcasting and the Ministry of External Affairs. It must be said that when the ministry does approve a script it gives the film-makers all possible support and help to make the film. However, when Malle's films were shown by the BBC in England the Government of India, because of the outcry from Indians living there, asked the BBC to stop the transmissions. They didn't like the image of India that was being presented; the poverty in Calcutta, vultures eating the bodies of dead cattle and so on. Indians are very sensitive – perhaps overly sensitive – to the image presented of them and their country. Nevertheless the BBC decided to show the films and as a result they were kicked out of India and not allowed back until some three or four years later.

Our own relationship with the ministry goes back to *The Guru*, our first Indo-American co-production, and we have never had any problems about script approval, although we have had our share of problems about import and export of equipment, raw stock, rushes etc.

I left Delhi for Jaipur on the 25th accompanied by Mr Amulya Ratan Kohli, a friend of Naushad Ali who keeps close contacts with the ministries and bureaucrats in New Delhi, particularly with the Ministry of Information and Broadcasting (where I had first met him) and the Ministry of Home Affairs. Mr Kohli was a bureaucrat in the Rajasthan Government some years ago and is a very close friend of Mr Rathore, the Deputy Inspector General of Police. On our arrival in Jaipur we were greeted by the staff of Deputy Inspector General Rathore and taken to his house. We discussed the controversy that was raging in the newspapers about *The Deceivers*.

The accusation being made against me was, apparently, that my film misrepresented Indian culture. I couldn't see how. Thuggee is a well-documented part of Indian history. Sleeman and his exploits, on which the novel is based, were not fiction. Neither is sati, which is one of the film's sub-plots. The film we were making was not an invention. More to the point, the novel had been available in India for some thirty years and had never caused any comment.

I have made many films in India and I had never met any official opposition in the past. On the contrary, people had gone out of their way to help us and we were always welcomed at the various locations where we prepared to shoot. It had been as if local people shared our pride in what we were doing; they felt they were a part of it. So the current attitude was not only foreign to me, but inexplicable. What pained me most was that I was being accused of misrepresenting Indian culture. One of the principal purposes of Merchant Ivory Productions coming into existence at all was to bring that culture to western audiences. To show India sympathetically had been the basis of several of our films in which India appears almost as the central character.

We all knew there was no valid reason for these objections to the film, but I had been made aware of two separate articles in *The Times of India* on 23 September which had disturbed me very much: they linked the sati which would appear in my film to a sati that had recently taken place in Rajasthan which had caused a tremendous uproar all over the country, with one side crying 'Shame' and the other – much smaller, but no less vociferous – maintaining that the suttee had been a blessed, even beautiful event.

In the first article Basant Vyas alleged that the script we had submitted to the Ministry of Information and Broadcasting was not complete and contained some 'crucial omissions'. Apparently several other organizations in the city had joined in the demand to ban the shooting of the film. In this article

Nick denied that we had shot scenes of orgies in a Hindu temple, and that we had filmed at Deorala, the village where the sati had recently taken place.

The second article, however, was a spirited defence of our film by Ranbir Singh, the chairman of the Rajasthan Chapter of the Indian People's Theatre Association, who demanded that the state Government should find out the credentials of Basant Vyas and the others who were objecting to the shooting of *The Deceivers*. He asked why these people had not objected to the sati scene in *The Far Pavilions*, and, if Mr Vyas felt so strongly about social evils, why he had not condemned the recent sati in Deorala. In Mr Singh's opinion the filming of *The Deceivers* was an important cultural event in Rajasthan, and he criticized the 'self-appointed guardians' of Indian cultural heritage for politicizing the issue because of what he called 'personal grudges and inflated egos'.

Nevertheless, in the first article we had denied there was a sati scene in *The Deceivers*. In view of the circumstances at the time I knew it was the right thing to do.

On 4 September Roop Kanwar, an eighteen-year-old widow, was made sati in Deorala, a village some sixty-five kilometres from Jaipur. It was reported that the young girl, numbed by grief, voluntarily climbed on her husband's funeral pyre. But later reports indicated that witnesses had seen the girl trying to run away and that finally, in what appeared to be a drugged state, she had been forced into the fire. Some fifty people from that community were arrested for abetting the sati and had been imprisoned to await trial. The events in Deorala provoked huge pro- and anti-sati demonstrations throughout the state of Rajasthan. Vyas and Mishra had apparently taken advantage of the strong feelings on the subject and used the sati scene described in *The Deceivers* screenplay to spearhead their campaign and gather support against the film. Although three weeks had passed since the sati, the story was still front-page news all over the country.

Sati is one of the most explosive issues in India today. It was outlawed by the British administration in India, but the custom is still alive, especially in remote or poor areas where an unsupported widow becomes an additional and un-welcome burden on her husband's family. Put simply and brutally, culture shrouds expediency in the myth that the act of sati is a woman's greatest virtue.

The name sati (in English suttee) comes from the goddess who sacrificed herself for her husband and thus became dei-fied. Today there are Hindu fundamentalists who hold that it is essential for a wife to keep her husband's honour and, in order to achieve this, she must die on his funeral pyre next to him. If she does so, not only is the honour of the deceased man upheld, but she in turn becomes a goddess. But it is very rare, none the less, for the widow actually to take this step.

To understand sati it is also necessary to understand some-thing of the condition of women in India and their position in society. From the start, daughters are not welcome. Every family hopes for a son, because a son is a permanent member of the family, later increasing it with his wife and sons. A daughter on the other hand is considered a guest: she does not belong to the family because she will be married and multiply and enrich her new family. Traditionally every daughter must be given a dowry on marriage, so she also becomes an econ-omic liability. Whether married or not, Indian women have few rights, beginning with the denial of the right to choose their own husbands.

I knew about the Deorala sati and the subsequent demonstrations. I had been in Bombay at the time, and the incident had been much reported in the national and interna-tional press. When I read about it I experienced the horror that, I believe, any rational human being would feel: first, that tradition and custom had made a young girl take her own life, then, with the subsequent reports, that she had been forced into the fire. Indian law regards sati as a criminal act, and the majority of Indians feel similarly. Most village women can do little to change their situation. Having had little or no education they wouldn't know how or where to begin. Their chief preoccupation, understandably, is looking after their children and seeing to their husbands' needs.

I was very surprised and unhappy that our film had become linked with the issue of sati The sati scene in our film was simply a vehicle to set the plot in motion: it was not a central feature of the film in the manner of the sati in *The Far Pavilions*.

On 24 September another article in *The Times of India* quoted the Rajasthan Pradesh Youth Congress as saying our film glorified the institution of sati, and went on to reveal how the production team had been assaulted by a group of rowdies who had also damaged our equipment. From the article it seemed that various groups were putting pressure on Harideo Joshi, Chief Minister of Rajasthan, to ban the shooting of the film and, rather disturbingly, the state Government had changed its earlier stance of defending the permissions and had started a process of stalling. Basant Vyas repeated his accusations that we had submitted to the Ministry of Information and Broadcasting a script that was incomplete and contained some crucial omissions.

These last two statements were completely untrue and I felt that people were out to malign reputations and distort facts.

I have always had a very good relationship with the press, both in India and internationally. Whatever they choose to write about me, I would always prefer to meet them face to face and discuss matters than have them resort to secondhand stories and gossip. They are a powerful force and there is nothing to be gained by antagonizing them.

By the time I got to the Rambagh Palace Hotel in Jaipur after my meeting with Deputy Inspector General Rathore it was very late. There were two men, along with a young lady,

The Nawab's caravan (Ramgarh, Rajasthan)

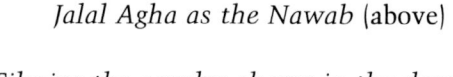

Jalal Agha as the Nawab (above)

*Filming the cavalry charge in the desert at
Tala, Rajasthan*

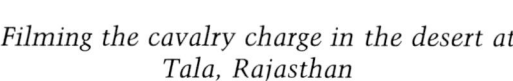

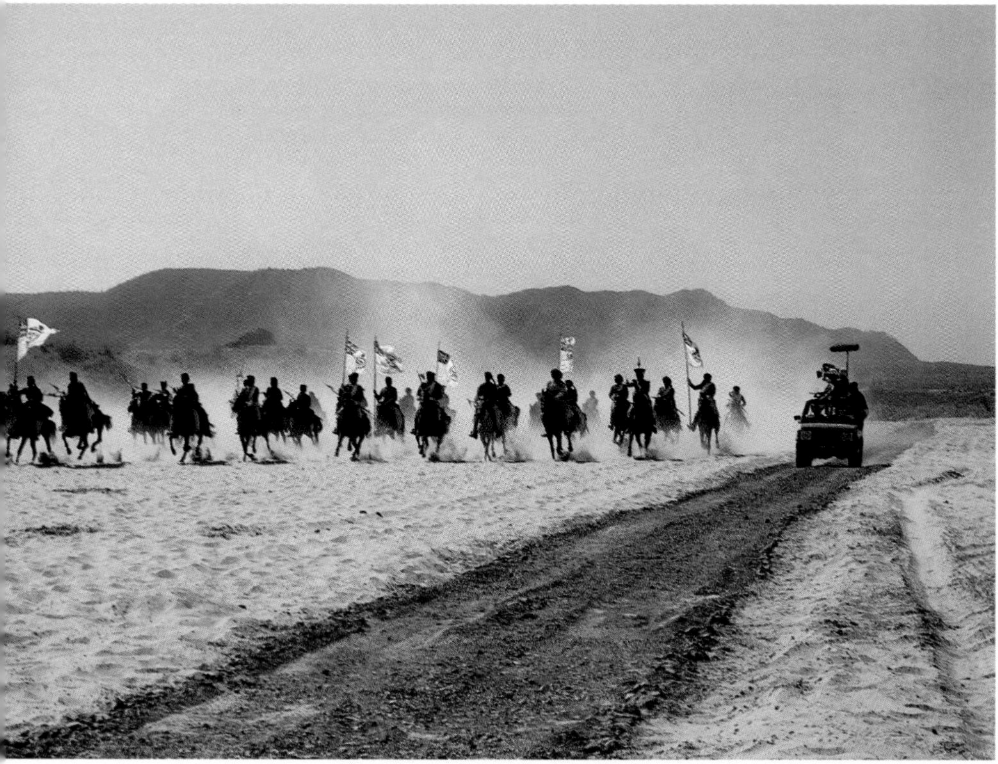

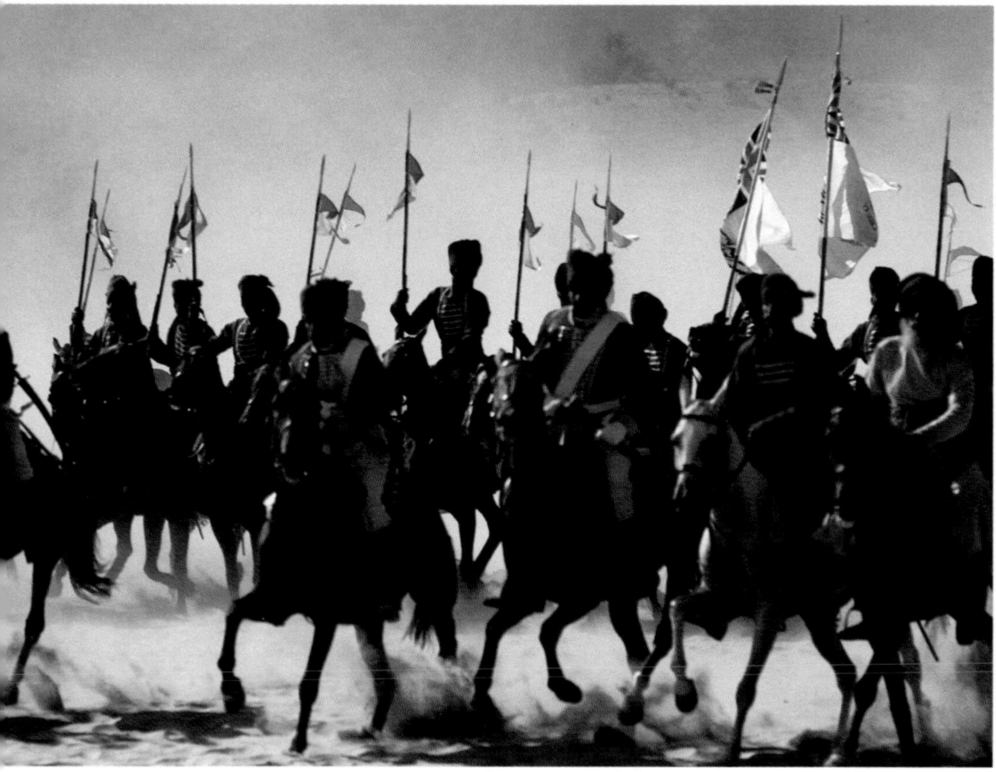

Extras on the Parsola set

*Parsola – the thugs gather to sell
the stolen jewels*

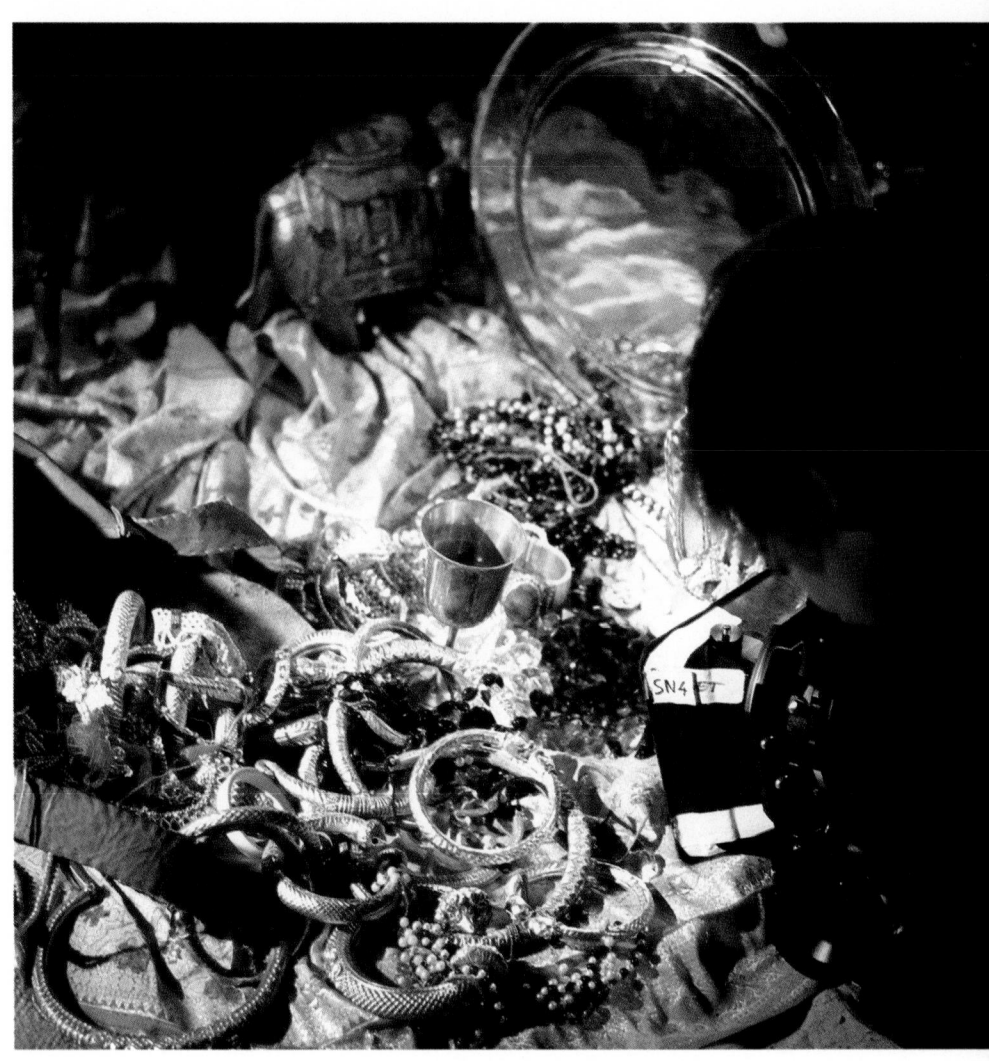

The $2-million-dollar shot (above)

*Gopal (Pierce Brosnan) threatens to kill Hira Lal
(Shanmukha Srinivas)* (right)

*With Tim van Rellim, Pierce Brosnan and Saeed
Jaffrey on the Parsola set*

waiting for me in the lobby of the hotel. Two were freelance journalists from the *Illustrated Weekly*, and the third was Mr Ranbir Singh from the Indian People's Theatre Association who had stoutly defended our right to make the film.

The journalists complained that earlier that afternoon they had visited our production office in order to interview me. They were treated badly and were thrown out of the office. I calmed them and promised to look into this rude behaviour, because I knew that now we had to be extra careful with the press.

Although it was late and I was tired, I answered their questions and tried to clear up the misinformation about sati and the cultural elements in our story. Aside from anything else, so many people had had their say about *The Deceivers*, I felt it was time for me, who knew more about the film and what it involved and didn't involve, to have *my* say. I denied emphatically the reports that we had filmed the *chunari manotsav*, the eleventh-day ceremony after the Kanwar sati at Deorala. That had nothing to do with our film and there would have been no reason to do it. In fact we could not have done so: our cameras had not yet arrived from England. I was very angry and upset by that accusation. I don't mind a fair story, but most of the reports in the papers about *The Deceivers* had been distorted. The script that had been approved by the Government of India was the shooting script and, as is the custom, the Government had appointed a liaison officer to be present on the set each day to see that we did not deviate from it. I reminded the journalist that we were the people who had made *The Householder*, *Shakespeare Wallah*, *Heat and Dust* and many other movies that centred on Indian culture, and never had the slightest objection been raised to anything in any of our films. Finally, because I felt it was time the public should know what I already knew, I told them that I believed the motive behind all these protests was not concern about Indian culture at all, but a concerted attack of one individual who had been denied employment on the production: Bonnie Singh.

With no possible justification for these protests I had felt that something more sinister was behind it all. It hadn't taken me long to discover that the two people spearheading the campaign were both involved with Bonnie Singh: Vyas was a good friend and Sunaina Mishra worked very closely with him. Singh and Mishra had been involved in and actively supported the filming of *The Far Pavilions*, and must have assumed that they would be involved with the making of *The Deceivers* as another foreign film. Except that I was no foreigner.

I think that if I had been in Jaipur from the beginning of this agitation I would have understood what was happening and have been able to stop it before it had gone so far. No one had made an effort to do public-relations work locally. Things were made worse by not speaking to the press, because that implied that we had something to hide.

Sunaina Mishra then issued a writ against us in the High Court of Jaipur. The charges she made in the writ were that the film 'depicts a wrong picture of our Hindu culture, religion and mythology. The goddess of Kali, which is a symbol and Goddess of power and worshipped throughout the country by millions, has been projected as "Demon God" as is evident from the extracts taken from the story ... The film depicts immoral acts, violence, vulgarity and does not show Indians (men and women) as being of good character.'

And so it went on. From now on, our film was daily front-page news in India. But the newspaper stories were often based on rumour. We were accused of desecrating a whole forest and violating the Wildlife Protection Act, of erecting electrical installations in rural areas (all we had were portable radio transmitters whose antennas were hitched onto our jeeps) and so on. I felt that some of the journalists were acting in an irresponsible manner and not checking their facts. They seemed to accept these rumours because the sensational nature of this sort of thing would sell more papers. Before we start shooting I always call a press conference so that everyone knows what we are doing and what is going on. I decided to call a press conference now.

Meanwhile, I asked our lawyer Jagdeep Dhankar to prepare an affidavit in reply to Sunaina Mishra's writ.

We had the document from the Ministry of Information and Broadcasting confirming that the modifications to the script had been carried out and the film was now cleared for shooting; a further document sent by the ministry to the Chief Secretary of Rajasthan asking that facilities to shoot in Rajasthan be extended to us; a document appointing the official liaison officer who would be on set for the duration of shooting to make sure we did not deviate from the approved script; and a document, copies of which had been circulated by the Government of Rajasthan to every official department in the state, from the Superintendent of Police to the Chairman of the State Electricity Board, requesting that they should extend their cooperation and assistance 'as per rules' to facilitate the successful preparation of the film in and around Jaipur.

We held a press conference at which we presented these documents, and prepared a press release which we distributed to the press and wire services.

Sunaina Mishra and party's case was heard in the High Court on 8 October and was dismissed by Justice S.C. Agarwal and Justice Pana Chand Jain. The judges observed 'that the petition was not maintainable and did not deserve any interference for relief by the Court. There was nothing on the record of the Court to convince it regarding distorted depiction of the Hindu culture or religion. As such, the petition deserves to be dismissed.' This news was relayed to us by the Deputy Minister Bina Kak at a youth gathering where we were being honoured.

Now, I thought, we could get on with making the film.

CHAPTER IV
CASTING AROUND

The political problems began to take up a lot of my time. I had decided to bear the responsibility of the court case myself. I wanted, as far as possible, to distance the cast and crew from the controversy, because I didn't want the quality of the film to be compromised. With the unit I treated the whole matter lightly: I didn't want them to worry about anything except the making of the film – and that, in itself, produced more than enough difficulties. There were $6 million, twenty years of dreaming and seven years of effort invested in this film, and I wasn't prepared to sacrifice one cent of that money or one second of that time.

As it was, I thought Mishra and her friends were doing everything they could to disrupt the filming as well as the film. A water-holding dam which we had built for one of the scenes had been destroyed and the water had drained away. We rebuilt it and again it was destroyed. Bolts were stolen from the camera crane, making it inoperable until we had new ones made, water was put in the generator fuel and many other mysterious things kept happening. We stepped up security, but it didn't seem to make any difference. What we didn't know at the time was that we had employed many people who were friends of Bonnie Singh's. We were working and living among spies. Even Bonnie Singh's brother-in-law, Raghvendra Singh, was working for us as Saeed Jaffrey's stand-in. Gradually we discovered these sinister connections and began to rid ourselves of people we suspected of being hostile to the film.

Beyond these matters there were the ordinary problems of film-making – or the extraordinary ones. The logistics of the exercise were awesome. In some scenes we needed to transport over 100 horses and more than 400 extras, as well as the huge film unit, deep into the Rajasthan desert. We had to supply food and, much more important, water, for all those people and animals. Open trucks and lorries carrying people and supplies could only travel as far as the edge of the desert; beyond that the vehicles would sink under their own weight into the sand, and it was impossible to dislodge them. From there, everything had to go by jeep, but even the jeeps often got stuck and had to be pushed. By the time the huge metal containers of drinking water reached the shooting site the water would be hot and unpalatable.

Other scenes involved elephants, donkeys, bullocks and all manner of livestock in similarly inaccessible or difficult locations. In Rajasthan the heat and the unrelenting sun caused the greatest suffering. Later, in the jungles of Khajuraho we had the additional dangers of the local wildlife: snakes, scorpions, poisonous spiders and aggressive monkeys (one bit Jenny, our costume designer). Wherever we went we took with us a fully equipped ambulance and two excellent physicians from Bombay, Dr Pankaj Pandya and his wife, Dr Deepika Pandya. Dehydration and heat-stroke were the most common problems, and there were one or two accidents but, surprisingly, very few people fell ill.

However, we had other problems common to all film-making. We had arranged for some young actresses to come up from Bombay for a scene in which the thugs are shown getting stoned on opium and are entertained by courtesans. These actresses knew before they came that they would have to strip, or partially strip, to create the right atmosphere. When the time came, however, their attitude was suddenly very prim. I could sympathize with them but, on the other hand, they *had* agreed to do it. In India, for all sorts of moralistic reasons, it's still uncommon to have nude scenes in films: the censor's code is still very Victorian. But it seems to me hypocritical because, although they don't shed their clothes in

Indian films, I think the suggestiveness of the Indian film stars' songs and dances is much more vulgar. I don't disapprove of nudity in the cinema – as our films will attest – although as an Indian I am aware of my countrymen's delicacy even in private life over the matter of nudity.

In the case of *The Deceivers* it may have been, too, that the film was perceived as being a foreign picture, and the actresses playing the courtesans disliked the idea of being naked on foreign screens, perhaps worried – like so many Indians – about their image abroad. Something of the same sort happened in *Quartet*, a film shot in France by us in 1980. French actresses refused to strip for a British picture! And of course the public opposition to *The Deceivers* was not exactly reassuring to these young actresses we had imported, who, according to the newspapers, were to appear in a pornographic movie.

We also had trouble with the hookahs which the thugs are supposed to use. We had special-effects experts from England and India, but none of them could get the hookahs to work. Then everybody started fumbling with them to make them start. I went out to the village and found two old men who were smoking and brought them to the set. In seconds they had the hookahs going. On a film set everybody is some sort of 'expert', but the producer has still to be more expert than anybody at speedy improvisation.

One of the problems that concerned me most was Nick's cavalier attitude to the details of Indian customs and behaviour, which he sometimes chose to ignore for the sake of getting on with the work, or because he thought a scene would look better, even if it was wrong. On the second day of shooting, for example, the scene where Savage and Hussein arrive at Hussein's home was filmed with the women of the house excitedly rushing out to greet the men. Muslim (or, indeed, Hindu) women would not come out of the house shouting and waving their arms and showing their faces because it just wasn't (and often still isn't) done. When I arrived in Jaipur I was told by Walter and also by Jenny Beaven that the scene didn't look or feel right. I watched the rushes on cassette and saw that, indeed, the scene was quite wrong and would have to be re-shot.

Normally during shooting the rushes are shown in a screening room at the end of each day. But because the import regulations of film rushes and magnetic sound into India are complicated and need special permits, as well as attracting customs duties, we had our rushes transferred to cassette and sent to us in Jaipur by courier.

One of the things that is often said about our films is that 'all the money is up on the screen', meaning that the budget has been spent on the picture rather than wasted on grand living off set. In fact, on most of our films what is on the screen is far more than the budget has allowed, and I can do that without going over budget. This is probably because I am what you might call a 'seasoned borrower'. It started in the old days when we couldn't afford to buy or even hire props, so I would borrow things from friends. When you make small-budget films the only way to put the kind of richness and opulence we seem to need on the set is by borrowing things, and sometimes I have borrowed things that can't be bought or hired. For *The Deceivers*, as for other films, and even though we now had a lot of money for once, I still borrowed all sorts of extraordinary things that weren't available for hire or sale. There is one scene in the film that, had we paid for the props, would have wiped out a third of our total budget. This was the scene where the thugs gather at Parsola in order to sell their stolen jewels. For this scene we needed some really impressive jewellery to make the scene look rich, and as Jaipur is the centre of the gem trade in India I didn't think I'd have too much trouble finding it. I went to the Gem Palace, a wonderful jewellery shop, and asked if I could perhaps borrow a bit of jewellery for the film. The Kasliwal brothers, the owners, filled up two old briefcases with about $2 million worth of jewels and brought them, without any form of security, to the set, which ended up looking on screen like Aladdin's cave. We had outdone Hollywood: our jewels were real.

I have known the Maharaja of Jaipur (who is known as Bubbles on account of the enormous quantity of champagne supposedly consumed at his birth) for some years, and while we were in Jaipur he invited me to tea. I took Ken and Letizia with me because I thought they would like meeting him at home – that is, in his palace. Ken saw there some antique lamps which were unique, and he suggested they would look perfect for a scene in the film. He asked me if there was some way we could have them copied, but I just asked Bubbles if I could borrow them, and he agreed. Ken was amazed.

One of the essential props we needed was a piano, and we had been warned that it would be very difficult to find an intact piano of the Regency period in India, so Ken was prepared to have the local cabinetmakers construct the shell of one. But there are always surprises in store, and things often crop up in the most unexpected places. While Ken, Letizia and I went hunting through antique and curio shops we also visited a shop specializing in old rugs which belongs to a friend of mine, Ramswaroop Vijayvargiya, an antique dealer who as a very young man started out in a modest way by going into business selling Rajput miniature paintings and drawings which came to him tied up in dusty old bundles. Vijayvargiya is now a leading antique dealer with a successful export business. Inside the shop old rugs were draped everywhere and, as we examined them, by chance we uncovered a rare rosewood Regency pianoforte that had been in India since the 1820s standing under a veil of dust and carpets, like a beautiful woman concealed in a shroud of shawls.

But not all of our problems were so easily or happily

resolved. Nick and Tim had hired Gerry Crampton as stunt coordinator. He had worked in India many times, usually on big-budget films like *The Far Pavilions* and the Bond films. The Stuntmen's Association in India has separate regulations and different rates of pay for Indian films and for foreign films. Stuntmen can earn triple pay by working on foreign films. Naturally, I wanted to avoid that because I didn't see *The Deceivers* as a foreign film. But Gerry Crampton who was acting as the unofficial Equity representative had already led the stuntmen into making the kind of demands they would make of foreign films and, in my eyes, they became very like the characters we were representing in the film. On one occasion Crampton objected to the make of vehicle that had been sent to collect his stuntmen. He refused to come on the set and just took his stuntmen and walked away: this delayed shooting by half a day. Crampton seemed to believe that his stuntmen were better than anyone else in the movie and therefore deserved to ride in limousines, which, in any case, we didn't have.

Nick had been persuaded that, as the thugs in the film would be riding horses and doing all kinds of stunt work, it would be sensible to have stuntmen playing some of the thugs, and he was assured that the stuntmen could perform as well as any actor. In fact we soon discovered that they couldn't: in one scene a thug, played by a stuntman, had to be strangled and thrown into water. To our horror, and his no doubt, we saw that he didn't know how to swim, and he had to be replaced, ironically, by an actor who could.

The casting of a film is always a fascinating process. Sometimes your heart is set on one actor to play a role and you just can't see anyone else in that part. But if that actor can't or won't do it, you always find someone else and, strangely, it turns out to be the best choice for the role, or so you feel. As is evident from our films, we like to cast new young actors and actresses whenever possible and it is particularly rewarding when they go on to establish successful careers for themselves, as so many of them have done. I felt that in Pierce Brosnan and Helena Michell we had very good casting for Savage and Sarah, Savage's wife.

After all the problems in finding the right combination of director and writer, I was relieved that the casting of *The Deceivers* had gone so smoothly. In casting the role of Sarah, we had considered many actresses and finally it came down to Joely Richardson and Helena. I would have been happy with either of them for the part. I had worked with Helena on *Maurice* and she had been excellent in the part of Ada. I had never worked with Joely (whose mother is Vanessa Redgrave) but I knew her and had seen her in *Wetherby*, which impressed me very much. We chose Helena, the final decision being Nick's. He thought she would be more compatible with Pierce. Neither of us had worked with Pierce, and nothing we had seen of his work demonstrated what he could really do with a demanding role like Savage. Yet once Christopher Reeve was out, I had always felt that Pierce would be right for the part.

Nick's forte as a director is his flair for story-telling. He seems less comfortable with characterization and atmosphere. Perhaps he is simply less interested in that aspect. But actors need to probe into the part they are playing. One of Jim's special qualities as a director is that he does give actors his time towards this exploration of their character, so the performances he manages to get from even inexperienced actors are more interesting and stronger than you might expect them to be. Nick, on the other hand, works out in his mind beforehand exactly what he wants his actors to do. But the best actors naturally have their own ideas about a part and how it should be played. The director has his vision, but it's the actor and the acting that finally bring that vision to life for the director. After the first week of work Pierce felt that Nick's approach might in time create constrictions for him because Nick wasn't allowing him any personal interpretation of the part. But gradually Pierce became very firm about how he wanted to play certain scenes and Nick had to bow to his actor's convictions, as directors have so often done.

By choosing Helena for the part of Sarah, Nick also indirectly solved another casting problem. In the film Savage's superior, Wilson, is also Sarah's father, and Nick thought it would be a great idea to get Helena's real father, Keith Michell, to play Sarah's father in the film. Father and daughter had a wonderful time working together, and Keith joked that he was delighted his daughter was now getting him work. They were both in India for the first time and went exploring whenever they could. On one occasion they took a rickshaw ride and the driver assumed that Helena was Keith's young mistress – and would not believe Keith's protestations that Helena was actually his daughter!

When we first approached Keith with the part of Wilson he had a previous commitment to play the role of the painter Augustus John at the Savoy Theatre in London's West End. The play was to have a limited twelve-week run, but after that he would be available and was happy to take the role. At that time our schedule was such that Keith wouldn't be needed until halfway through the shooting, which coincided with the end of his play, so he was offered a contract. I was hesitant about finalizing the deal until after our recce in India, when we could confirm the schedule, which was still uncertain, but Nick insisted on settling the contract before the recce. Originally both Ken and I wanted to shoot the tiger hunt in Khajuraho, but there were difficulties about the availability of elephants and we had to shoot that scene in Jaipur, though that was a mistake from the point of view of location and both Ken and I were unhappy about it. Worse than that, however, was that by shooting the tiger hunt in Jaipur we would need

Keith earlier than we had anticipated. We asked the producers of his play if they would be prepared to release him, but they were not at all keen. We had a firm contract with Keith which we would have to fulfil: according to Jean Diamond, Keith's London agent, the change of schedule was our problem and not Keith's. In the event, however, Keith's play closed before its full run, as it had not done as well as expected, and Keith just managed to get to India before the tiger hunt.

I was pleased that Saeed Jaffrey was to be in this film, playing the part of Hussein, the thug who is captured by the British and who later takes Savage to join the Deceivers. I have known Saeed from my very first student days in New York. He was then married to Madhur Jaffrey, and I took an instant liking to both of them; they became a part of my life and they have remained so. Saeed had established strong connections with the New York theatre, as well as radio, television and music, and I admired him. I went to plays with the Jaffreys, saw films with them and spent many enjoyable evenings in their company. I was very sad when they divorced.

In 1980 Saeed had had a leading role in Satyajit Ray's film *The Chess Players*. Suddenly Saeed, whose career had been established in England and America, found he was in great demand in India and began doing more work there. Saeed's second wife, Jennifer, who used to be a researcher at the BBC, enterprisingly set herself up as a casting agent in Bombay, and it was she who was responsible for finding many of the Indian actors for *The Deceivers*. She brings the kind of forthright, western approach to her work that is essential for a casting agent, applying standards of selection which western directors working in India appreciate and must rely on.

Without doubt Jennifer's greatest coup on this film was finding Shanmukha Srinivas, who plays the part of Hira Lal. We needed a graceful young boy with an exquisite and innocent face, who would also be able to dance, and we looked everywhere. In Delhi we went to the Kathak school of Briju

Maharaj, a celebrated Kathak dancer, but found no one there who looked right. Then just three weeks before shooting, Jennifer saw in one of the Indian trade papers a still, from a south Indian blockbuster film, of a young boy gliding through a temple. She contacted the producer of the film and arranged for us to see this eleven year old who, we discovered, was not only making ten films simultaneously but was also a precociously gifted physics scholar at college! Shanmukha arrived with his father and completely enchanted us all with his wonderful dancing and singing.

The part of Chandra Singh, the Indian nobleman and friend of Savage's who, unknown to Savage, is also a thug, was taken by Shashi Kapoor. Shashi was in our first film, *The House-holder*, and has been in three subsequent films. Shashi's father was the Indian actor, director and producer Prithviraj Kapoor, a legendary figure very prominently involved in both theatre and film. Our relationship with Shashi goes back to 1961 when I was taken by the late Betty Delgarno, an Australian friend of mine living in Bombay, to a party at Shashi's house. Shashi had just made his first Hindi film, *Char Divari*, which was about to open, and he had invited some journalists to his home, where Betty and I gatecrashed his party. When I arrived I recognized some of the journalists whom I had met when I was organizing my variety entertainments at college while I was still a student. Shashi was very charming, pleasant and hospitable towards us. We took to each other instantly and started chatting as though we had been friends for years.

Since then we've worked together and shared so much of our lives that the Kapoors are now *my* family. We have watched Shashi's rise and his decline and then his rise to even greater heights – for the popularity of movie stars is as unpredictable as the weather. And he, too, has shared our disappointments as well as our triumphs.

It was through Shashi, who was married to Jennifer Kendal, that I met the Kendal family, who were in many ways the

William (Pierce Brosnan) and Sarah (Helena Michell) travel on horseback to his station (Acherol, Rajasthan)

Feringea (Tariq Yunus) 'thugs' Gopal
(Pierce Brosnan)

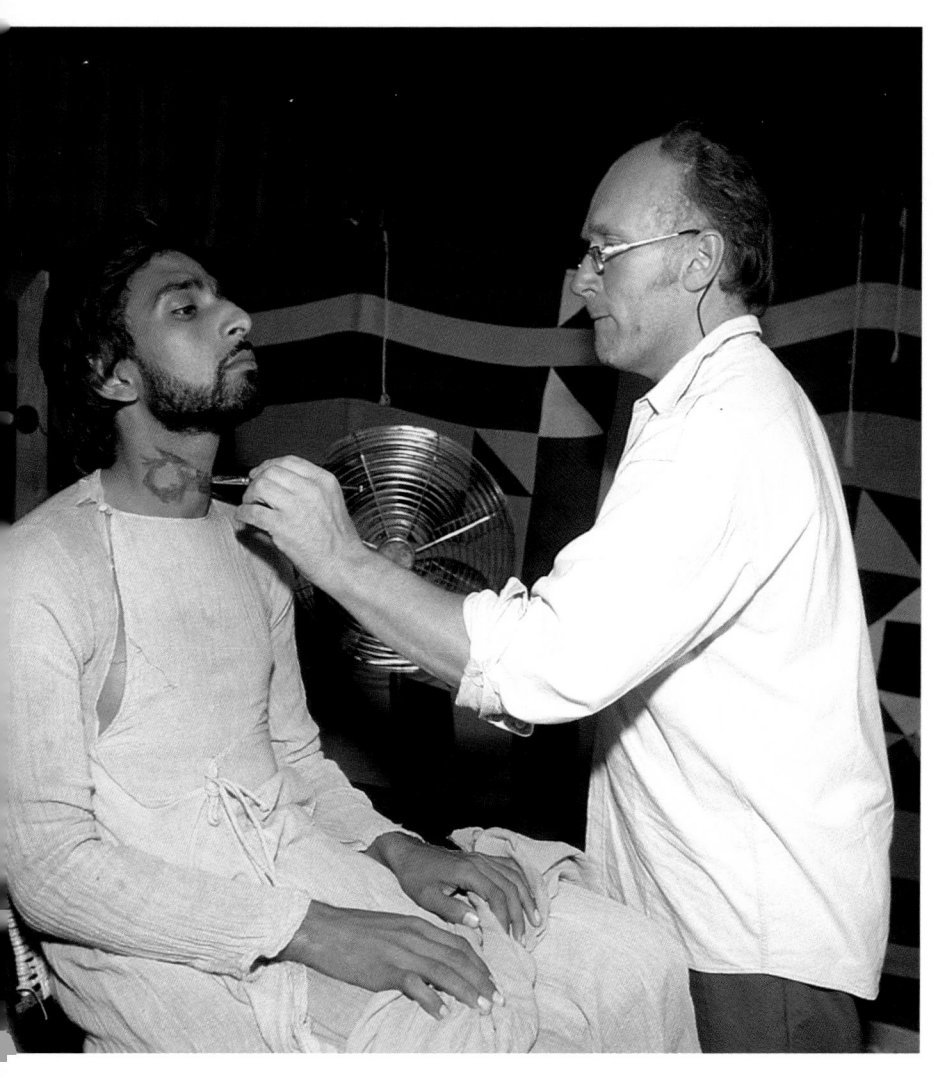

*Make-up artist Colin Arthur creates a
'strangled' effect*

(Above) *Filming the travellers across the river (Kukus, Rajasthan)*

(Below) *Cooling off (Tala, Rajasthan); Nick Meyer directs the bullock cart through the river* (right)

*Gopal (Pierce Brosnan) attacks one of
the travellers*

The travellers attempt to fight back

Rajesh Vivek as Duleep Ram, the thugs' holy man

inspiration of our second film, *Shakespeare Wallah*, which established Merchant Ivory as film-makers. We used all the members of the Kendal family in that film, which starred Felicity Kendal, then only eighteen, in her first screen role.

Whenever I was in Bombay, I used to have breakfast with Jennifer and Shashi. It was peaceful to go there and sit down to chat. I enjoyed those visits so much. Jennifer died recently, and it is hard to come to terms with that. I have the feeling that she has gone on a long journey and I am still waiting for her to come back.

CHAPTER V
KHADIM

On the first free day I had, a Sunday, I went to the city of Ajmer – a three-hour drive from Jaipur. Ajmer is the burial place of Khwaja Mohinuddin Chishtie, over whose tomb a large shrine has been erected. He has been our family saint for a century. My father, my grandfathers and my great-grandfathers from both sides of my family drew inspiration from the saint who is believed to have had miraculous powers and is honoured among both Muslims and Hindus. Many pilgrims come to Ajmer hoping to have their wishes fulfilled, and when these prayers are answered there are often huge celebrations at the shrine, around which many poor people live who must depend upon the charity of the pilgrims.

Ajmer has a very special significance for me. After my mother had given birth to three daughters she went to the shrine and prayed for a son, tying, as is the custom, a red-and-yellow ribbon on the Khwaja's tomb. I was born on 25 December 1936 – the answer to a prayer. My father thereupon arranged a great feast for all the people at the shrine. I know that my faith and my strength have been drawn from that saint, and I credit the success of my career to Khwaja Mohinuddin Chishtie's intervention. Part of my mother's wish was that I would be a *khadim*, a dedicated server of that saint. Now this *khadim* – I hope I may be considered that – was going to intercede with the family saint for the successful completion of the film, and to be rid of the antagonistic elements that surrounded the production. And, as always, I asked the saint's blessing for my family and friends.

Strange and powerful influences surround us. When I go to the shrine of Khwaja Mohinuddin Chishtie I know I am being blessed by the extraordinary powers that are commanded by the saint.

Ajmer is crowded and noisy, but the shrine itself is a place of peace and calm, full of wonderful memories for me. At a shrine like this – of which there are several in India – class and caste and even religious differences are discarded, something I thoroughly approve of. Race, caste and class should not be encouraged by religion, any more than they should play a part in film-making.

Everyone has heard of the Indian caste system, of its rigidity and of its tenacious hold on life as it is lived in India even amongst enlightened people, and of how the caste system, which is a Hindu phenomenon, is mirrored in other Indian communities, which have their own internal caste systems, just as rigid, in terms of social mixing, marriage and the professions, as that of the Hindus.

A film unit is similarly caste ridden. There is the 'emperor', or director, at the top: he may be mad or he may be sane; he may be benign or he may be a despot, but it does not matter. People are ranked under him according to their importance and according to their function, like medieval society. Imagine, then, what it is like when the natural despotism of a film company operates within a context of social hierarchies like India's. And imagine, too, if that film company, at work in India, is predominantly British with, among the British members, old notions that die hard of race and imperialism. There must have been some who were still nursing a secret longing for the governing apparatus of the defunct British raj.

There were Englishmen – think of them as the equivalents of the officials in the old Indian Civil Service, as Collectors and sub-Collectors and so forth – who, during *The Deceivers*, never stopped complaining about the Indians or patronizing them. They shouted and swore at them, accused them of being incompetent and of making costly mistakes. It was an attitude they held onto until they flew home from the Khajuraho airport, and even when they were safely back in

London. But the reality was that the British couldn't take one step on this film or in India without the Indians. This they never understood or faced up to. It was the Indians who had to drive them around, barter for them, negotiate deals, interpret for them and placate other Indians bent on tripping them up. The English crew members would have been impotent without them, yet they all too often strutted around like Kipling's little tin gods, wearing unbecoming and undignified short shorts, as no Indian in a comparable position of authority would have.

When bad manners and disdain for Indians are the predominant tone taken by those in positions of the highest authority, that same tone will be found amongst the lower ranks, who ape them, but more crudely. An offender in this way was the English production accountant, who had come to India with his computers to show us on *The Deceivers* the latest accounting techniques. But his methods of work with, and his attitude to, the Indian cashier, Kareem Kazi, whom he called 'Sooty', were of a sort that one had supposed went out with Independence in 1947.

We first experienced these attitudes during the making of our film *The Guru* in 1967, which was in some ways a similar kind of production: it had a big budget, for us at that time, and there were English technicians of a secondary importance working under Indians, who were often their actual bosses, and whom when filming in India I generally chose to trust out of loyalty and friendship.

By some fortunate mix of chemistry this kind of ugliness did not occur during either *Hullabaloo Over Georgie and Bonnie's Pictures* or *Heat and Dust*. You stand to lose more than you gain by discriminating against whole classes of people. If I were to reject an artist because of his race or his creed I would lose the talent of that artist, and I would be the poorer. In the arts, fortunately, discrimination is less prevalent than elsewhere: everyone is judged on the merit of his work. But there is something set dangerously astir when the English go out to one of their former colonies to make films, so this important fact is lost sight of. And perhaps India excites these atavistic feelings more than any other place due to the peculiar love–hate relationship between the British and India. While the English have a secret yearning to control, to be in command, we Indians feel compelled to look for slights at their hands; to hunt for grievances and, stubbornly and just as stupidly, to strike attitudes.

These mutual antagonisms had been simmering since the start of shooting, so it was not surprising that at some point the situation would come to the boil. I had had a complaint from the actor Tariq Yunus about Tim, and I asked Tim not to provoke Tariq. I like Tariq very much and I enjoy his company off set, but I cannot deny that he is sometimes more hot-headed than I would wish. Tariq is a Pakistani actor who has been living and working in England for many years. He is not just an excellent character actor but also an intelligent and imaginative one. As Feringea, one of the chief thugs in the film, he has to look very menacing and he thought up the idea of having a gold front tooth which he would reveal very slowly in a sinister smile, a brilliant touch that appealed to Nick.

I know that Tariq had asked for a bed in his dressing tent because he has a bad back, and Tim had refused on the grounds that Tariq was not a 'star'. Whether someone is a 'star' or not, I believe everything should be done to make the actors as comfortable as possible. Tariq didn't make a fuss about it, and Pierce kindly offered him his own bed, which he never used. But the slight – not an imagined one – rankled with Tariq.

I had gone to Bombay to organize some things for the film and on my return to Jaipur I heard some disturbing news from my assistant, Ben Barker. That morning Tariq's driver had arrived late and Tim's eighteen-year-old daughter, Natasha, who was working as a runner on the film, was very rude to him. She shared Tariq's car to the location, and for the whole forty-minute drive she shouted and swore at the driver for being late. Tariq asked her to stop because, apart from anything else, the driver didn't speak English and couldn't understand what she was saying. But she didn't stop and Tariq lost his temper and began shouting in turn at *her*. By the time they reached the location she was in tears and ran to her father to tell him how beastly Tariq had been to her. Tim launched a verbal assault on Tariq, who by now had had more than enough of the Van Rellim family. Tariq boxed Tim in the face and Tim went down. Tariq pulled him up and hit him again. He would probably be beating him still if people hadn't rushed to stop him.

I was very sorry when I heard about this, a first on a Merchant Ivory film. I went to the set and immediately encountered Tim. I told him how strongly I disapproved of what had happened. Michael White, recently arrived in India, had been to see Tariq. He had tried to calm him down and put him in a better frame of mind, but Tariq was very upset. When I went to see him he said, 'Boss, I'm not sorry it happened, but I'm sorry it happened on your film.' I, too, was sorry it had happened on my film.

Tariq was due to leave halfway through the shooting to make a film in England and planned to return to India later to complete our film. The day of the incident was to have been his last day of work before he left for London, but he had arranged to stay for two more days because he wanted to throw a big party for everyone, to celebrate his birthday. However, when he went to the production office the following morning to collect his air ticket he found that he had been booked to leave that very day. When he told me what the production office had done, I asked him if he wanted me to rearrange things. Frankly, I didn't think it was a very good idea to have a party at that time. Tension was running high.

Fortunately, I didn't have to say any of this to Tariq. He thanked me for my offer but rejected it for those very reasons and left the same day. Some of the production people were already predicting that Tariq wouldn't come back and we would be stuck, but I knew he wouldn't let me down, and he didn't. Later the mild-mannered Pierce pretended to be very angry with Tariq – not because he had boxed Tim but because Pierce had missed seeing it.

I was not in India during the pre-production stages, and the mistakes that were made then I had to pay for later. I dislike going somewhere to make a film and flashing money around and making a big noise about it. I prefer to be discreet and keep a low profile. But it was not to be on *The Deceivers*, and I think our film became a victim of all the show and glitter and glitz that movies are usually associated with. I had tried to establish that unity with the local people which has always been a feature of our film-making in the past, but under the circumstances it was very difficult. I don't like to come to a place as an outsider and find myself working against the locals. I like to have personal contacts with the traders who supply goods, the people who offer their services and all the others who are in any way involved. And this applies most of all to the people who are working with me on the film: the actors, the crew and the technicians. I don't want to work with people who are only doing a job for the sake of the pay cheque at the end of the week. I want them to be directly involved in the film and be committed to it and to enjoy the whole experience of making it with us. That is extremely important to me, and with that attitude the wheels turn in a completely different way to the way they were turning on *The Deceivers*.

Of course we have frequently had problems of personality

on our films in the past; it would be unrealistic not to expect them: certain tiresome individuals, problems with union representatives and their more gung-ho members – none of that is unusual. But never in my experience have I had to face the problem of 'camps'.

By now, however, camps had certainly been formed. There were those people that Tim had brought into the production, who owed him loyalty. Then there were all those that I had hired – and Tim's actions showed he resented them. These antagonisms had surfaced earlier when Michael White and I understood, mistakenly, that Tim had resigned from *The Deceivers*. Tim claimed the support of those he had brought into the film and acted as if he were suspicious of anyone he had not personally vetted. He took no trouble to hide his dislike of my team, and an uncongenial atmosphere was soon created: while professional behaviour carried on normally, there were always underlying tensions.

Tim's sense of his own importance matched his notion of *The Deceivers* being a 'big production', as opposed to the previous 'small' Merchant Ivory productions: 'little' films like *Heat and Dust* and *A Room with a View*. He resented interference from me because all my experience came from these small-scale pictures. Yet what was the truth about his position in the film? Simply, that he was hired to be a line producer, taking his orders from Michael and me. He had absolutely no power or control beyond what we assigned to him so that he could get on with the job. To be fair, leaving his unfortunate manner aside, he was very good at organization and highly efficient in matters of logistics; the production always ran smoothly, and at the end of the day we always achieved what we had set out to do. But with his 'big production' mentality came a tolerance for 'big-budget' kinds of waste. And there I stepped in to 'interfere', for we were ending up overpaying both in salaries and for suppliers. Apart from anything else, by overpaying for local labour we made things difficult for Indian film-makers, who cannot pay the kind of salaries outside film-makers pay. There is a local rate for employment on films and, although it might not seem much by English or American standards, it is, for India, a very fair rate. I knew what those rates ought to be. They had kept up with all the other rising costs of film-making in India, of which Tim had no experience.

I think most of the problems that came up were the result of my not being on the spot when the production was being put together, or on the set as much as I like to be. Because of the American opening of *Maurice* at the beginning, and the local agitation about the film, which escalated day by day, I had to spend a lot of time away from the set. Internal problems mounted and, as I was not there to deal with them, they either weren't dealt with at all, or else they were dealt with in a way that just caused more problems later on. I think the next time I make a film I shall first have a robot made in my image and leave it on the set if I have to go away: it will be wound up and set going. The eyes will flash red, the arms will wave and terrifying noises will be heard.

I wanted to get away from all these petty and frustrating things, to forget all the unpleasant business and just have some fun, as we usually do on Merchant Ivory films.

There is a wonderful scene towards the end of the film, of the cavalry charging through the Rajasthan desert on its way to the rescue of Savage. The 61st Cavalry, the last surviving Indian mounted unit, is of course very impressive to see, as well as being very tough. The 61st has appeared in films before, but won't any longer, unless it is within its authentic historical context, which wasn't the case in our film because the 61st didn't exist in the 1820s. Fortunately they were prepared to overlook that particular rule for me. They stuck out the burning 114° heat for two long days, as if they had been on a real campaign. The cavalrymen wore the heavy red woollen coats of the period and the British officers were in their stiff dress uniforms. I hope that when the members of the 61st see the film they will feel the results justify all their discomfort. It was a spectacular sight – a hundred men galloping against the sun in a mist of sand, pounding hooves and lances flashing in the blinding white light.

We found out too late that one of the two cameras used for the cavalry charge had malfunctioned. The heat and the daily treks on the rough roads to and from the locations had taken their toll on the camera equipment. We would have no idea of whether the film had been badly affected by the problem until the report of the rushes was sent back from London. We would have to wait for three days, and by that time we would have lost the 61st, which would no longer be available for shooting. Meanwhile, a mechanic was sent from London to repair the malfunctioning camera.

Each day our rushes were sent to London for processing. The laboratory reports from Technicolor would indicate the technical quality of our footage and whether or not we had any major problems. So far, the technical reports had been very reassuring, and even more encouraging were the responses from people like Paul Bradley, my associate in London, to what they were seeing in the screening room. He sent back increasingly enthusiastic telexes praising the photography, the performances and the over-all production values.

At this stage of making a film, I have found that it is generally more productive to criticize than to congratulate. If things don't look quite up to the mark at rushes, or ideas aren't working, there is still time to put things right and improve what you are doing. But because all the people seeing the rushes in London and New York were as aware of that as I was, I knew their responses were genuine and that the results were as impressive as I had always known they would be. Even as you are shooting the film you may get an idea of what the visual impact will be on screen. It is less easy to judge the performances of the actors. Because of the fragmented way a film is shot, you can judge the quality of the acting in a particular scene, but you can't really tell what the over-all effect will be until you begin to put the film together and are able to see how the actors have shaped their performances with the director to create characters. In our case we could only judge the effect of what we were doing by viewing the selected rushes on VCR in Nick's hotel room. But it was enough for me to see that, at the very least, *The Deceivers* was likely to be hailed as one of Walter Lassally's best works.

But, like all films, the rushes contained farcical moments, too. After the cavalry charge Chandra Singh, played by Shashi, runs until he is finally caught and killed by Wilson, played by Keith Michell, who is on horseback. Dramatically, this is one of the high points in the movie, with the thugs scattering through the long grass in a mad panic to escape, and the English horsemen riding them down one by one. The first take went very well until the moment when Keith was about to kill Shashi, at which point the horse began, most undramatically, to graze at Shashi's feet. On the next take Shashi's moustache fell off. The third take went beautifully, but just as Keith was about to plunge his sword into Shashi, his horse backed away, leaving Shashi still very much alive. At first it was funny, but I could see that gradually people were becoming a little tense in the heat. After another failed attempt Shashi cried out, 'Kill me, kill me! For God's sake, please kill me and get it over with! Anything's better than this torture.' Everyone laughed and I shouted back at him, 'It's no use, Shashi, even the horse knows that you are a great movie star, so he keeps his distance!' Eventually Keith skewered Shashi, to large sighs of relief from the unit.

I felt a similar relief when I received the report of the rushes from the cavalry charge. They were good: only a few takes had been affected, and there was more than enough footage for our purpose.

While the 61st were confronting thugs on film, my own enemies had not disappeared. A few days after Mishra's petition had been defeated in the High Court I received a letter from Himmat Singh of the Rajasthan Film Production Society – an organization, according to the letter, for the promotion of film production in Rajasthan. He referred to the problems we had been having as a 'created misunderstanding' and offered to act as a mediator between the two sides. I was amazed when I read that letter. I knew that both Sunaina Mishra and Bonnie Singh were members of the society and I couldn't imagine what the motive behind the offer was.

Mishra had lost the case, and I supposed the only reason she wanted a reconciliation was so that I might stop giving interviews to the newspapers in which I might give information that would possibly discredit them and thus affect their chances of obtaining further work on foreign film sets. I was prepared to meet with them because I generally have no objection to meeting with people, but we never had that meeting, because in the meantime, on legal advice, I had filed a counter-suit against Mishra alleging obstruction of lawful business and defamation, which was something they had not foreseen.

I felt I had to sue. I had worked for twenty-five years to build a solid reputation, which they had tried to impugn by accusing us of being anti-Indian, of manufacturing pornography and, most irresponsible of all, of utilizing a tragedy for our own commercial ends. I was not interested in revenge or the nominal damages I was claiming, but there is too much of this sort of double-dealing in India today, and I wanted to show these people that this time they wouldn't get away with it. They could not lightly make these false claims, and then having made them live as if nothing had happened. They must be made to face the consequences of their own actions, and I hoped it would stop them from trying their antics on other foreign film production companies as well. As an Indian I don't want people coming to my country to make a film and leaving with a bitter taste in their mouths.

A rose-petal seller at the shrine of Khwaja Mohinuddin Chishtie, in Ajmer (above). With Nayeem Hafzika outside the shrine (below)

The bungalow at the Rajasthan Polo Club, Jaipur

Interior of the bungalow

With Helena Michell

*George Angelsmith (David Robb) watches the
sleeping Sarah (Helena Michell)*

St George's Cathedral, Agra (above)

*Inside the church (above right): the wedding of
William and Sarah; (below right) George
Angelsmith (David Robb), William (Pierce
Brosnan) and Sarah (Helena Michell)*

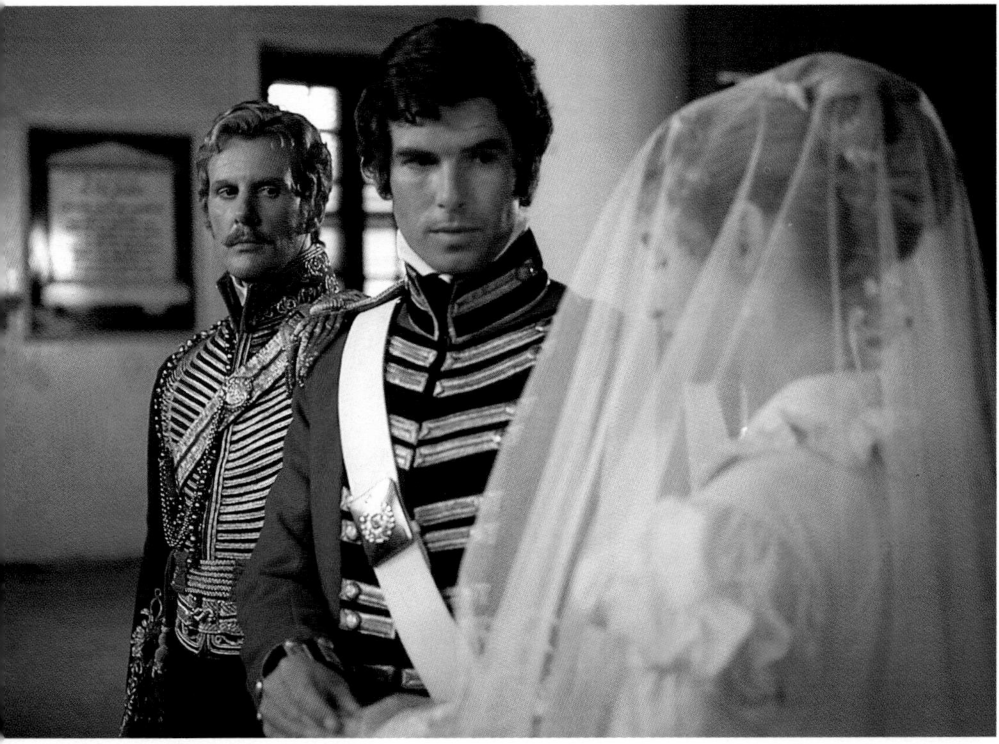

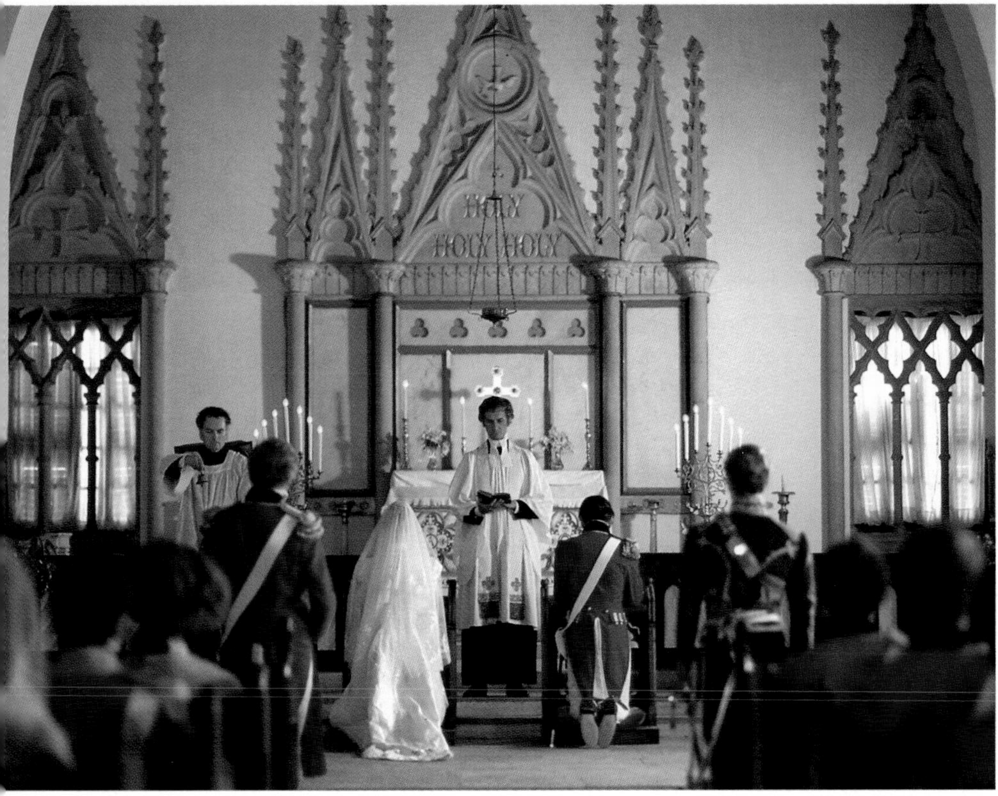
HOLY
HOLY HOLY

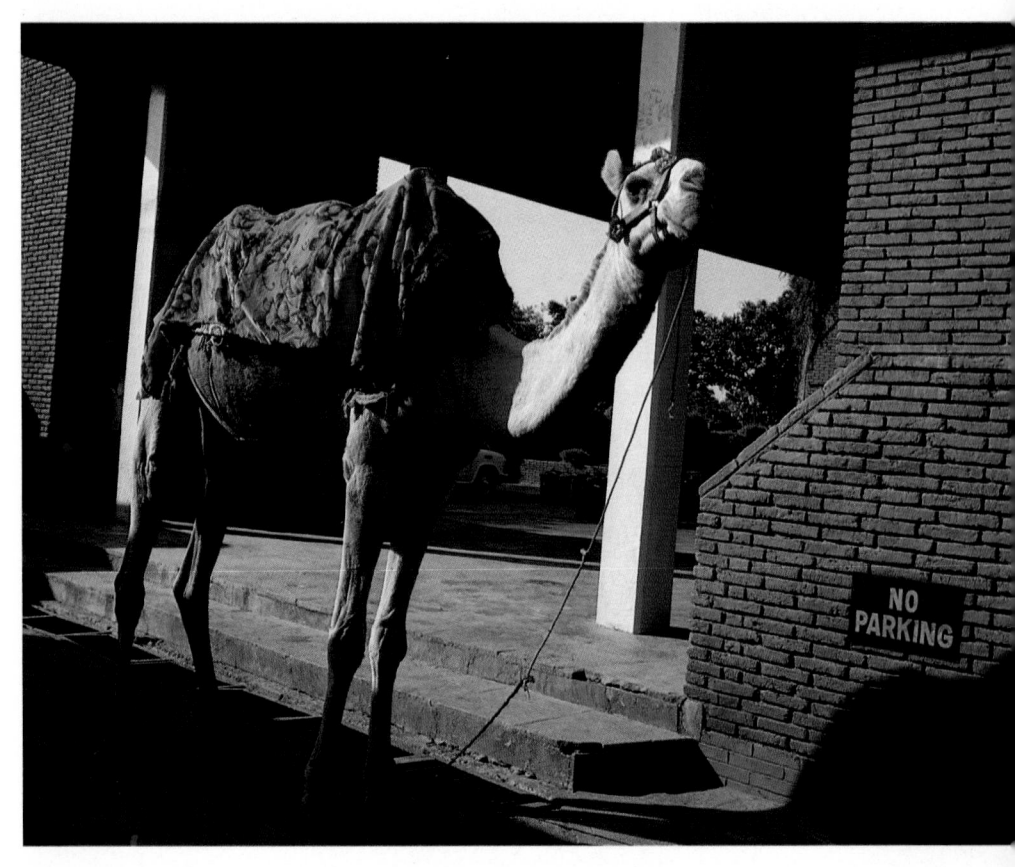

Traffic violation (Agra)

CHAPTER VI
SPLIT SCREEN

Locations have always been very important to us. When we began making films we couldn't afford to hire studio space or to build expensive studio-type reconstructions, so we made all our films on location. What had been dictated by necessity soon became our preference. I think that location shooting gives a film an authenticity that no studio reconstruction can match. I also believe that the actors benefit by being in the appropriate place, and the atmosphere on the location does affect their performance.

We have been to some extraordinary places and have shot in many wonderful buildings, most of them normally inaccessible to film crews. But whenever I find a perfect location for a film, I will move heaven and earth to shoot there; something which usually demands enormous finesse in negotiations. However, I believe it is significant that our reputation is such that we have been granted access to places denied to other worthy film-makers.

When we were making *Maurice* we wanted to use E.M. Forster's own college, King's, in Cambridge. It was the appropriate place and our hearts were set on it. We knew that King's had never allowed a film to be made there, and we were also aware of how many worthy applicants had been rejected in the past. I argued to the trustees at King's that the film *had* to be made there; it would be Forster's wish, and so forth. In the end they did allow us in, and many senior academics, distinguished dons – some of whom had known Forster – appeared in the scene during formal Hall where Clive Durham recites the Latin grace.

When I began planning *The Deceivers* I knew exactly what I was looking for. There had to be a variety of locations throughout the film, because I wanted a significant contrast between the landscape of Savage's home and the landscape of the denouement. I wanted to show how far Savage had travelled geographically, which would also imply his psychological journey. I wanted him to travel from a lush, green, and gentle landscape to a brutal and terrifying one. It was for this reason that we chose to film both near Khajuraho and in Rajasthan. Nick's and Ken's enthusiasm for these locations made me very happy.

The exteriors and the Indian interiors would not be difficult, but the British interiors, I knew, would present a problem, because little is left of the original British architecture of that period. I knew of St George's Cathedral in Agra, which was built in 1827, within two years of the period of the book. I felt that it would be perfect for the film's wedding scene. While I was in Agra checking out the church I came across the Agra Club, a building which not only offered the right setting for the ball and Wilson's study but – always important to me – could also accommodate our production offices during our short stay in Agra to film some of the interiors.

The greatest problem was finding a British bungalow from the early 1800s for Savage's home. Although Agra had an army post and a large British cantonment dating back to 1870, and there were many British bungalows as well as churches and clubs, most of the surviving bungalows are of a later period and so would be inauthentic, and the one or two bungalows dating from the earlier period were in ruins or so altered as to be impractical for shooting.

In Khajuraho we found a bungalow on the banks of the river which was an ideal location because we had more or less settled on Khajuraho as Savage's home territory, and parts of Rajasthan as the major setting for the thugs. But, although the Khajuraho bungalow was in the most appropriate place, it was not convenient for shooting because it was too small and had been modernized. The possibilities began to look bleak, and it was then that Ken came up with the idea of constructing a bungalow ourselves. I was worried that the cost of such a scheme would be prohibitive until Ken explained that, by building a bungalow large enough to accommodate the camera movements, actors, crew and equipment, the filming would be unrestricted by technical considerations and we would, in fact, save a day's shooting. So sometimes when you want to save money it's better to spend it; that's something I learned from Ken. One should always be receptive to good ideas and have an open mind.

Although in theory Ken's idea was good, in practice I knew that in Khajuraho it would be difficult to find the right materials and the experienced labour for the work that building the bungalow involved. The most practical solution was to build the bungalow somewhere in Jaipur, where all the materials and skilled labour would be easily available, and hope the surroundings would pass for Khajuraho.

It was Ken who decided on the Rajasthan Polo Club as the site for the bungalow. Fortunately the Polo Club belongs to Bubbles, the Maharaja of Jaipur, and he agreed to let us use a part of the golf course. Ken designed the bungalow and it turned out magnificently – everyone fell in love with it and wanted to live there. Because the ground surrounding the bungalow was burnt out and dry, we recruited local help to dig up whatever sparse blades of grass could be found and re-plant them individually around the bungalow. It was a back-breaking and time-consuming process, but eventually the bungalow was surrounded by a lush green lawn. We brought in trees and bougainvillaea in full flower until the garden finally resembled an oasis in the middle of a desert.

Rajasthan was suffering from terrible drought, and the expected monsoon failed to materialize for the tenth successive year. Water was still available in Jaipur, but conditions in some of the villages were very serious, and it was forecast that by the end of the year Jaipur, too, would suffer. I was very conscious of our own demands for water on their limited resources. We called on the Chief Minister of Rajasthan, Harideo Joshi, and gave him a cheque for Rs50,000 towards the Drought Relief Fund. At the presentation the Deputy Minister of Culture, Bina Kak, introduced us to the Chief Minister. There were photographers, television crews and newspaper reporters trying to get the minister to talk about suttee and the controversy about it in his state of Rajasthan. Our small contribution was accepted and appreciated by him. Bina Kak then invited us to tea at her residence nearby.

Everyone was aware of the drought problem and Colin Arthur, the make-up assistant on *The Deceivers*, started a collection among the unit for money to build a water pump at one of the villages where we had been shooting. The response from the majority of the cast and crew was so generous that he collected more than enough money for the pump, and the rest was given to charity.

Once we had solved the major problem of the bungalow, we then had to create the interiors. India, with its long-standing British links, is an excellent source for western antiques; and although pre-raj pieces are rare, we discovered all kinds of antiques and period furniture (including the Regency piano). Some things we found locally, other things we brought in from Bombay. With Bubbles' permission we raided his palace from the attics to the cellars for props and furniture and other objects. What we couldn't find at antique dealers, or in the homes of friends, we had made. Ken, impressed by the standard of craftsmanship in India, told me he didn't think we could have achieved those results anywhere else in the world. It was a perfect recreation of an Anglo-Indian administrator's house at the beginning of the nineteenth century, and was furnished down to the last details of white muslin punkahs and hanging glass-bell lanterns.

Ken had brought with him two Italian assistants, Franco Fumigalli and Rafaelle Vincente. I think God gave the gift of design to the Italians. They have such a good eye, such superior conceptual gifts and finesse in execution. When

Gianni Quaranta, one of the production designers on *A Room with a View*, won an Oscar for that film, I was not in the least surprised.

Letizia Adam became a major asset in preparing the bungalow for shooting. She was indefatigable in her searches through the bazaars of Jaipur for the right fabrics, resourceful in communicating with her Indian upholsterers through flamboyant Italian gestures when language failed and infinitely patient in getting everything absolutely right. She is a striking woman of great character who in her white *salwar kameez* and enormous straw hat would look as fresh and elegant at the end of a long and dusty day as she did when she first came on set in the early hours of the morning.

In the crowded, noisy bazaars she and I would sift through piles of fabric, and I was amazed how she could immediately visualize how appropriate something might look on the set. Like Jenny's costume makers, Letizia's upholsterers sat in the open, working and re-working the cloth on old manual sewing-machines until every seam and braid was stitched to her exacting standards. No imperfection, however minor, escaped her notice and she made a great deal of noise until something was exactly right, and then made even more noise praising and hugging her loyal workers. Like Ken, she never complained about anything and never lost her sense of humour or her sense of proportion. During one minor crisis, she was apparently in deep and serious conversation with Anna Kythreotis, a Greek journalist friend of mine who was there on assignment. But they were not talking about film crises. They were discussing the origins of the derogatory term 'wop', and whether it should be applied to Greeks as well as Italians, Italians in general, or just Sicilians. 'At a time like this,' Ken said to me as he looked at their intense and serious faces, 'they are discussing etymology.'

For a month we had been shooting in the countryside around Jaipur. Because of the distances involved in getting to the locations the unit often had to be on the move by 5 a.m.

Early starts, late finishes, long journeys and gruelling working days in intense heat left no time or inclination to socialize. When we started shooting the bungalow sequences in the city, life became a little easier. Those staying at the Rambagh Palace Hotel could walk to work across the grounds of the hotel which adjoined those of the Polo Club, and no one was more than a few minutes' drive away. As the filming came to an end in Jaipur several parties were arranged by the crew. One was given at the Raj Mahal hotel where some of them were staying. The Raj Mahal used to be one of the Maharaja's palaces and it is very grand, with a beautiful garden and pool.

When I arrived I had noticed that inside the hotel, in one of the ballrooms, there was a *mujra* in full swing. Once a month some local businessmen get together at the Raj Mahal and invite musicians and singing- and dancing-girls to entertain them. I hadn't heard good singers or seen good dancers for a long time and, although these performers weren't particularly good, I just didn't feel in the mood for the shop-talk at the unit garden party. Although I went to our party, I could not resist the lure of the *mujra*. Traditionally only men are allowed to enjoy a *mujra*, which is fundamentally performed by courtesans. The girls are there to sing and dance and the men are there to appreciate and be entertained. A lot of money changes hands on such evenings. You give the girls money when they sing, for the exceptional poetry of their songs; when they dance, for the exceptional grace of their dancing; and for everything else they do they are offered money, the presentation of which is as elaborate, as dictated by etiquette and the right timing as all the other aspects of the evening. In time, everybody always gets very drunk. Dinner isn't served until well after midnight and the whole thing goes on until the early hours of the morning. And of course the entertainment doesn't necessarily end even then; more intimate entertainments may follow elsewhere, as I showed in my film, *The Courtesans of Bombay*.

This kind of entertainment appealed to my mood that night, so I took Saeed (who is always ready for a *mujra*), Mikki Ansin, our stills photographer on the film, and Anna, and we crashed the businessmen's party. Indian women are not normally expected to attend a *mujra*, and I wouldn't think they'd want to anyway. The courtesans can behave more freely in the exclusive company of men. But they don't mind foreign women – they just think, 'These *ferengi* women, who cares?' When Mr Alhuvalia, the manager of the hotel, saw me he very graciously invited us, officially, to take part in the celebrations. The mood was charged with drunken souls, and the courtesans were applauded at every gesture and movement of their hips. Even the *ferengi* women I had brought with me joined in, much to the delight of the men and the amusement of the courtesans. Some other members of the crew joined us, and it was almost daybreak by the time we left. Saeed didn't want to leave at all, because he said he had fallen in love with *all* the courtesans. We had to carry him out. Fortunately the next day was a Sunday and he could sleep it off.

I had especially enjoyed taking my friends to the *mujra*. Mikki had got so carried away singing and dancing with the courtesans that I decided to play a joke on her. When we got up to leave I told her she had to stay behind because I had sold her for $6 million. At first she didn't believe me, but I finally persuaded her that it was true. She looked absolutely horrified as I said goodbye and walked away. She pleaded with me to give the money back, but I told her it wasn't possible, and I kept the joke up for as long as I could, with Mikki getting more and more distraught. On our way home she confessed that she really felt quite flattered that I had supposed she was worth as much as $6 million.

I have always enjoyed introducing my foreign friends to an India they would not normally see. I have never wanted to be a man of one country. Whilst still retaining my own culture, nationality and religion, all of which are a part of what I am, I want to live everywhere and make films everywhere and not be bound by any national or cultural barriers. Although I have now been established in the west for nearly thirty years, I never 'emigrated'. I don't feel as though I have *left* India. I am, and always will be, Indian. I have Indian nationality and an Indian passport and I don't want to change that. India is my country.

Everyone sees India through different eyes. Tourists and visitors see it as a place of extraordinary natural and man-made beauty; the mountains and lakes of Kashmir, the sweeping coastline of Goa, the great palaces in Rajasthan, the Taj Mahal; others see it as a country with extreme problems, poverty and the slums of urban cities – Calcutta in particular; politicians exploit it for all the wrong reasons. I see it as the place of my roots, the place where I was born and I grew up, a place I love and return to as frequently as possible. All my family live in India. It's a huge family: I have six sisters and so many nieces and nephews I've almost lost count; every time I go back there seem to be more. My father died very suddenly in the autumn of 1986. He had seen the success of *A Room with a View* and I was glad of that. I had had a very liberal upbringing and I was free to do whatever I wanted with my life, but I knew he had hoped I would enter the legal or the medical professions: secure, profitable, respectable professions.

I will probably never enjoy that kind of security, that kind of respectability, but at least my father had seen me successful, respected and happy in the field I had chosen. He was very ambitious for me, and both he and my mother gave me the best education they could afford and certain social advantages. But beyond that they left me alone to do what I most wanted and to go wherever I wanted.

How much time I spend in any one place is governed largely by whatever film we are working on, but I seem to spend more and more time suspended in mid-air. However, travelling is part of my work. I have to go to many different places and meet a variety of people, so it is fortunate that I am able to assimilate so easily. No place has ever felt foreign nor have I ever felt like an 'outsider'.

Yet at the same time I still *feel* Indian. There is one national characteristic, however, that I do not share with my countrymen: fatalism. I have always been an optimist, even during my worst hours, of which there have been quite a few.

There is a huge conflict in the Indian character. In general the people are straightforward, hard-working, hospitable, open-hearted. Yet at the same time there is an extraordinary streak of violence running through Indian life at all levels. India is not a peaceful country and never has been. I was eleven at the time of Partition and I still remember vividly the riots and the anger and the hatred. I still wonder at how so much hostility and rage can burst forth from such outwardly docile and gentle people. It horrifies me that something so demonic can emerge from religious sentiments. Religion is such an integral part of India's life that anything can trigger off the most dreadful violence. Politicians are constantly exploiting this situation. I dislike religious extremes as much as I dislike heartless materialism.

The single most radical influence of the west on my life has been through its artistic culture. I was aware of western culture but I was not familiar with its refinements. I knew something of English literature because the English classics were part of the curriculum at school and college, but I had no knowledge of European, Russian or American literature until I came to the west. Even Nirad Chaudhuri and Ruth Jhabvala I first read in America. Western art and paintings I had only ever seen reproduced in books: I had never seen an original canvas in a gallery or artefacts in a museum. These discoveries were like a new dawn. But the most surprising discoveries for me were European cinema and classical music, because I simply wasn't aware that either existed. The only western music that reached India in the fifties, when I was growing up, was popular music, like rock and roll, and ball-room music because ballroom dancing was very popular amongst the affluent classes. There were a great many clubs in Bombay – the Cricket Club, the Wellington Club, the Radio Club – and every week they would have a formal dance evening. I was taken to these clubs by a friend of mine, Mohamedali Bootwalla, who was very fond of dancing, and so I also came to learn ballroom dancing. But I had no idea there was such a form of dance as ballet, or that there was such a form of music as opera, until I went to New York.

The first things I saw there were *Swan Lake* and *Don Giovanni*. These were my introductions to ballet and opera and I was thrilled. Then I began to go to concerts. All these revelations were like suddenly being given a gift. And today I still feel I am being given gifts.

Western classical music influenced me so much that when I directed a short film, *Mahatma and the Mad Boy*, in 1972 I chose, as the background music, the Winter Concerto from Vivaldi's *The Four Seasons* – played on Indian instruments. I had considered the same idea for *The Deceivers*, not only to reflect the cross-cultural theme of the story, but also because of my own enthusiasm for both musical forms. I felt that Richard Robbins was the only composer who could accomplish this link of eastern and western motifs that I thought was essential to enhance the atmosphere of the film.

CHAPTER VII
ARRESTING DEVELOPMENTS

Although Sunaina Mishra and Basant Vyas had lost their case in court, I didn't think they would let the matter rest there. It's like the seven-headed cobra – you can chop one head off, but another springs up, you chop that off and a third appears. The very fact that they had lost the case meant that they would be spurred on to fight the film in some other way; it's that kind of mentality.

Their immediate move was to begin pestering the Government-appointed liaison officer from the Ministry of Information and Broadcasting, Bhagwan Mirchandani. One morning he came to me and told me that he was getting mysterious telephone calls in the middle of the night, from people who asked him all kinds of questions about the film: whether this or that scene had been shot, whether he had observed this or that. He told them that he was observing what the Government had asked him to observe, and beyond that it wasn't his job to ask any questions as long as the shooting was following the script that had been approved by the Government. He added that if they had anything to say on the matter or any questions to ask, they should address them directly to the ministry.

And that is what happened. The ministry received letters complaining that the liaison officer wasn't doing his job properly. As the ministry continued to support Mirchandani, the threatening calls began again, making Mirchandani's life a misery.

Mirchandani had a very interesting interpretation of the sati in the book. His theory was that as the widow believes that her missing husband is dead and she wants to join him, her immolation on the pyre is suicide. She does not become sati because, according to Hindu custom, sati can only take place when the dead husband's head is laid on the widow's lap and they are burned together. So it could be argued that there is no sati in the film, only a suicide.

The truth is that the sati (or suicide) scene was in the script from the very beginning, and the Government had approved it. They had no feelings about it one way or the other because they were aware that the story is set in 1825 and the sati is something of a sub-plot in the film and in the original book. Bonnie Singh and his crew had worked on *The Far Pavilions*, whose plot centres around a sati They did not object then. My feelings were that if they wanted to do anti-sati social work they should go out to the villages and preach to the people in Rajasthan not to succumb to this barbaric custom in the twentieth century.

When we denied to the press that there was a sati scene in the film we did so because we were becoming victims of the real sati. We knew the Government didn't object to that scene, and if it were done with subtlety it should not cause unnecessary concern.

What was also apparent to me, and what I had been warned about, was that the uproar surrounding the Deorala sati and all the fuss over our film was being deliberately stirred up to divert attention from far more important political issues in Rajasthan at that time. I was told that if our controversy passed into the hands of political people, which is what was gradually happening, it would be very difficult for us to finish the film. Fortunately, political machinery moves very slowly in India and the short shooting schedule worked to our advantage in this case.

I had briefly left Jaipur to meet with some of the local people at Khajuraho and smooth the way for our arrival there. In the state of Madhya Pradesh guns are the law, and I had been warned about the dacoits, the bandits of the region. I was hoping to leave all our troubles behind us in Rajasthan. I didn't want anyone from the unit being kidnapped and held to

The Agra Club – terrace

Betty and Joy at Khajuraho
(above)

One of the temples at Mausania,
Madhya Pradesh (right)

Props drying in the sun at the Rajgarh Palace
(above left)

Making decorations for the Durbar Hall scene at the Rajgarh Palace (below left)

Letizia Adam examines Chandra Singh's throne
(above)

Taking the corpses to the killing groves

William (Pierce Brosnan) discovers the bodies

Shashi Kapoor as Chandra Singh

ransom, because by the time the law or the Government get involved it is usually too late, and film shoots cannot be delayed for anything.

Lokendra Singh, the son of the Maharaja of Panna, was our contact man in Khajuraho. He is a wonderful man with a great sense of humour, and he is very well-connected in Khajuraho and Panna. Despite his name, he is not related to Bonnie Singh, though he is also of Rajput descent. I had met him through Betty and Joy Judah, two German-Jewish sisters who settled in Khajuraho many years ago, and who are the only permanent foreigners in the town apart from Betty's husband Gil, a Swiss.

The two sisters run the Raja Café opposite the main tourist attraction, the complex of temples famous for their erotic sculpture. The café belongs to the Maharaja of Chattarpur and is the social and cultural centre of the town: everyone goes there – tour guides, bandits and princes. Betty and Joy know everyone, and everyone knows Betty and Joy.

I wanted to make sure everything was done properly in Khajuraho, so that we wouldn't have the problems we had in Jaipur. Together with Lokendra Singh I went to see the Collector of Chattarpur, the place where we would be doing most of our shooting, and the Superintendent of Police. The Collector told us that the Chief Secretary at Bhopal, the capital of Madhya Pradesh, had written to him and had asked that all facilities should be extended to us.

The following day we made a similar call on the Collector of Panna and his Superintendent of Police, both of whom were very helpful and offered us their cooperation. The police superintendent later telephoned me and said that, through their investigation department, he had heard a rumour that there might be problems for us. The local member of the Janta party, a lawyer by profession, had been advised to watch what we were doing in Khajuraho closely, as he had been told the film we were making was derogatory of Indian culture.

The Janta is the opposition; the people's party. It was formed only a few years ago from many minor opposition parties for the sole purpose of ousting Mrs Gandhi and the Congress party from power. It succeeded in defeating Mrs Gandhi, but it then fell apart because the party members could not reach a consensus on any further goals. I keep abreast of Indian politics, and therefore knew that the Janta party is relatively lightweight, but I recognized that nothing would be gained by antagonizing it.

While I was away in Khajuraho, Mishra made her next move. She could not file another case against us in the civil court without further evidence, of which she had none. So now she pursued the case through the criminal courts, while not disclosing to the courts that a previous civil action had failed. The charges were obscenity, creating a public nuisance and – it sounds absurd to say it – swearing at Mishra. (Swearing at a woman in public is, if proven, a criminal offence in India.)

So far, the problems we had had in India had been reported only in the national press. The events of that night made international headlines. Anna Kythreotis, my Greek journalist friend who lives in London, had come to Jaipur at my invitation to write about the making of *The Deceivers* for the English newspapers. She was on the spot when thirty policemen armed with machine-guns came to raid our offices and arrest Tim and me. She filed the story, which was immediately noted and discussed in the British and American press in the next few days, resulting in a great deal of attention for the film. It was a journalist's dream, for most on-location stories about films being made are manufactured puff pieces. This was a real story.

The police had arrived at Kamani House, our headquarters in Jaipur, late on the night of 23 October, with a search warrant and arrest warrants for Tim and myself. Tony Waye insisted on reading the warrants before letting the police into the building and this gave our people inside Kamani House time to gather up the scripts and other documents relating to the film and take them out onto a terrace in order to hide them. There was nothing incriminating in the documents that were hidden, but we couldn't afford to have our shooting script and administrative schedules confiscated as evidence for any length of time. One of Mishra's complaints was that we hadn't deposited a script with the Government of Rajasthan. As the central Government had a script, this was not required by law, but we had, for the record, given copies of the script to both Bina Kak, the Deputy Minister of Culture, and Mr Bhatachariya, the editor of *The Times of India*, Jaipur.

Anna, who had a jeep outside, was given a bundle of scripts and documents and made a dash for it. She returned to the Polo Club with news of what was happening at Kamani House; everyone was very shaken by what they heard. There were a few moments of indecision until Nick announced that they would continue with the shoot. Those at the Polo Club were unsure of the details of what exactly was going on and who, in fact, was being arrested, so everyone was very nervous. The tension was palpable; every noise took on the nature of a menacing threat. The unit tried to make contact with Kamani House on the radio transmitter, but for a long time there was no reply. When they did finally get through the message was terse and to the point; no one must return to Kamani House that night, but go directly to their hotels.

I was told that Tim had slipped out by a back door when he saw the convoy of police jeeps arriving. Finding nothing else, the police finally took a few stills that were lying around the office. Meanwhile, Michael White arrived while the police were in the middle of their search. Amazed at what was happening there, he took some photographs, as he had his camera with him, to record this extraordinary moment. The police had behaved with civility and politeness despite their rather foolish mission, but at this point they seized Michael's camera and destroyed the film. At the time all this was happening I was sitting on a train coming back to Jaipur from Agra.

The first I heard of the incident was from Walter Lassally early the next morning on my way to have a swim. 'Well, that's fairly dramatic,' I thought when he told me. It didn't worry me because these kinds of things do happen in India all the time, though rarely in connection with a film. At that time it was just another problem I had to tackle: I had no idea then of how dangerous and tenacious the problem would become. I had breakfast with Michael White, who told me the whole story all over again. I wished I had been there. I relished the idea of confronting the police, and was disappointed at not being able to give a performance. Such upheavals are a bit like fighting the elements. You show what you are made of. But of course this was no tragedy; the whole thing seemed to me more like a farce.

However, I was concerned that Mishra would go so far. As the original case had been thrown out of court, I wondered how any magistrate could pursue an order of arrest. In fact the police had first arrived in the afternoon with a search warrant and Tim threw them out of the office. By handling the matter in this way Tim had inadvertently made the situation more volatile. When the police returned in the evening to arrest us, they expected resistance and trouble and they came prepared for it.

The next day was Diwali, the Festival of Light. Diwali is the Hindu New Year and a national holiday. The courts would be closed for the next five days. If the police were to return with the arrest warrants, there would be nothing we could do until the courts reopened.

Jagdeep Dhankar, our lawyer, explained that it wasn't just a matter of the courts being closed; the arrest warrant also effectively kept us in Jaipur. Neither Tim Van Rellim nor I could leave the city until the matter was settled by the courts. But in three days we would finish shooting in Jaipur and the unit had to move to Agra. Dhankar immediately organized bail for us, even before the arrest warrants were served. But although we wouldn't have to go to prison we could not leave Jaipur without the permission of the court, and the appeal could not be heard until after the Diwali holiday – or so it was assumed.

Dhankar went to the Acting Chief Justice that very day and pleaded an exceptional case for a special hearing, which was arranged to be heard on Saturday, the day before I was due to leave for Agra. The police officer came to present my arrest warrant and I had to sign it. I had piles of boxes of sweets in my office to distribute on Diwali to guests and friends, and I gave the police officer a box for his family. He was overcome by that. He told me that he was presenting me with my arrest warrant reluctantly, but it was standard legal procedure and had to be carried out – technically at least – because I had already been given bail.

I didn't feel like a criminal because I had committed no crime. That was what made it so silly: that I had not done anything that was a criminal offence and yet I was being charged with one. I was never treated like a criminal but, all the same, I had to go through the same procedure as I would have done had I broken the law.

I wasn't in the least concerned by the charges, though perhaps I should have been, considering the stubbornness of my opponents. The charge of pornography was demonstrably false. Every one of our films would prove that we are not pedlars of pornography, and *The Deceivers* is no exception.

The charge of creating a public nuisance is debatable. Does

making a film amount to creating a public nuisance? Certainly when Shashi made his first appearance on set in *The Deceivers* there had been a riot, but it was a friendly one. He is one of India's best known actors and crowds of people follow him everywhere. The parties who were campaigning against our film said that we had disrupted village life. But whenever you make a film on location you cause disruption – not just in a village in India. When we went to Cambridge to shoot *Maurice* we shot in the middle of term. We were using the college rooms, corridors and dining halls and, although we tried to be as quiet and self-contained as possible, inevitably we caused some disturbance to the students' and Fellows' day-to-day lives. It was the same with *A Room with a View* in Florence. We were there at the height of the tourist season and we had to block off the Piazza Signoria, which is one of the city's major tourist attractions, and forbid thousands of disappointed tourists to enter it. I always try to handle these matters as delicately as possible. You pay for the privilege of shooting on location, but money isn't everything. You enter into the lives of people and, yes, you do disrupt them, so you have to be polite and gracious and extra careful. In India when you enter a village with forty vehicles and hundreds of extras you shatter the normal calm of the village and change its whole character. The people have probably never seen a film being made and are naturally curious. But could what we had done be called a 'nuisance'?

As for the third charge – swearing at Mishra – that would have been very difficult for me to have done, as I have never met her or spoken to her. To this day I have no idea what she looks like. During the court proceedings Mishra was to say that she came to Kamani House, our headquarters in Jaipur, on Sunday 18 October to plead that we stop making this anti-Indian film. In response to her request she claimed that Tim and I called her names and abused her. At the time all this was supposed to have happened I had already left Jaipur for Delhi. Although I had never met her, we still had to prove in court that she was lying. This would not be easy because her 'witness' was Bonnie Singh's brother-in-law, who had been working on our film.

I was later told that some of these charges carry a two-year prison sentence – so they do have teeth. I took the news philosophically.

In the television documentary made about us, *The Wandering Company*, which Channel 4 broadcast in 1985, Ruth alluded to my unconventional methods of operating, especially with money, and confessed that she was always expecting to see me behind bars. Well, it looked as if her prophecy might be fulfilled, though not for her reasons.

So I began the New Year with a prison sentence hanging over my head. As a Muslim I don't observe Diwali as a religious festival but like everyone I love to enter into the spirit of the celebrations. On the day, we gave the 61st Cavalry the traditional gifts of boxes of sweets, and we also presented them with a video recorder and television in appreciation of their superb work on the cavalry-charge scene in the film. Colonel Sodhi and his wife Nafisa invited us to a firework display at the barracks where we presented them with our gifts.

The unit had to work on Diwali day, but all the Indian members of the crew were given the choice of taking the day off or working for extra money. The majority chose to work because they realized that we had only two more days to finish the Jaipur sequences and there was still a lot to do. I was grateful to them.

The Maharaja had asked me to invite some people from the film to the City Palace for the celebrations, so I took about twenty friends who I thought would appreciate the occasion and who, I hoped, the Maharaja would find interesting. Most people, of course, had not come to Jaipur anticipating such an event and began frantically searching for something to wear. Letizia Adam, who had struck up a wonderful relationship with the local upholsterers with whom she had been working to furnish the bungalow, took some fine Indian chiffon to them and, stretching out her arms in a pose, told them, 'All right. Now upholster this old chair.' They did. And she looked stunning.

By nightfall the whole of Jaipur was ablaze with candlelight and fireworks – a Diwali tradition. Every house, every shop, all the streets were lit by candles and oil lamps. The exploding fireworks made the dark sky glow with cascades of colour. The city was wide awake, and everyone went out in the streets to celebrate. All the shops stayed open, because it's considered lucky to start the year by making money.

The City Palace, the Maharaja's enormous Jaipur home, was blazing with candles and lamps. All the Indian guests were very formally dressed in *sherwani* or Jodhpur jackets and *saba* turbans. Because the Maharajas used to be carried everywhere on palanquins, there are no stairs in the palace, so we walked up shallow ramps to one of the terraces at the very top of the palace gardens below us, just as in an Indian miniature painting, where people are seen standing on the roof of a palace pointing at gold pinwheels against the sky. The final flourish was an explosion which blazed out the message: 'Happy Diwali'.

We were next taken through the gardens with their elaborate ornamental pools to another part of the palace. I don't think my guests had ever seen anything quite as grand as this palace, for it *is* a very imposing place – even the terraces and outdoor passageways that night were spread with fine Moghul carpets. From the vast crystal chandeliers overhead to the silk carpets underfoot, with the huge rooms extravagantly painted and gilded, it is exactly what people imagine a Maharaja's palace should be.

We sat and played cards, because everyone plays cards on Diwali. It is traditional to gamble on that night and if you win it means you start your year with a good omen. I won Rs140. But even Diwali was not without a certain amount of tension, I realized, as I faced a serious question of protocol. The Rajmata of Jaipur, the Maharaja's stepmother, Gayatri Devi, had also invited some of us to the Diwali celebrations at *her* palace. There is something of a family rift between stepmother and stepson. Since I've known them both for a long time and like them both very much, we split the group into two and went back and forth. At both parties there was of course a lot of talk and laughter over the arrest warrants and search warrants – situations that this particular Jaipur family has had a certain amount of experience with themselves in the recent past. In 1975, income tax officers broke into the underground storeroom where the Maharaja's inherited treasures were kept hidden and brought charges against the royal family for non-disclosure of income.

After cards at the Maharaja's we had dinner in a magnificent dining room at a table that could seat 150 people. In the old days when the Maharaja used this dining room there would have been a footman behind every chair. Now a great feast had been prepared for us and, though on a grander scale, it really looked like a scene from one of our films. It reminded me of the Nawab's dinner-party in *Heat and Dust*. At the end of the Diwali dinner, footmen brought in huge silver bowls for the guests to rinse their hands.

That evening everybody was drinking and we were all in a very jolly mood. We left at about 1 a.m., when I realized that I hadn't organized any transportation to take us back to our hotels. We walked into the great courtyard of the palace and at that moment a car appeared and the driver asked if we were his passengers. He was obviously looking for someone else, but I said yes, we were his passengers, and we got into the car.

So we took a joyride home, driving through the streets that were still sparkling with lights and people. I wanted to buy some silver, because it is a good omen to buy silver on Diwali, and special silver Diwali coins are minted for this day. Many of the shops were still open, but the silver shops, unfortunately, had shut, so there was nothing left to do but go home to bed.

The following day was the last day of shooting in Jaipur and the packing-up had already started at Kamani House. I didn't know what would happen at our Saturday hearing or, indeed, whether I would be allowed to leave Jaipur. The situation was ridiculous, but there was no question in my mind of not respecting the law; I had absolutely no intention of leaving Jaipur without the permission of the court. The last thing I wanted was to be in contempt of court, so I was prepared to follow all the procedures in the proper way. I already felt privileged because of the special dispensation that had been granted to have our appeal heard on a public holiday. I don't think that's something that would have been done for many people. But Jagdeep Dhanker, our lawyer, had told the Chief Justice about our background, about our films and also that Merchant Ivory was a respectable outfit. He was also made aware of our tight shooting schedule. Under those circumstances the Chief Justice had agreed to hear our appeal.

On Saturday morning I went with Jagdeep to the private chambers of Justice Gumnam Lodha. Justice Lodha was a very courtly gentleman with an imposing presence. He heard our case and he decided to suspend the detention order, providing Tim Van Rellim and I each posted a bond of Rs20,000. We had to track down Tim and bring him to the court because it was essential for him to appear and sign the papers in front of the Clerk of the Court.

I was absolutely delighted and got up and offered my hand to Justice Lodha and thanked him. He was very correct and told me that he did not shake hands and he did not deserve my thanks because a court of law is above thanks and such gracious exchanges, so he could not, he said, extend his hand: he was only executing his duty, and his duty was to see that justice was done. I was very impressed by this.

By the time we found Tim, posted a bond and signed the court papers, the Chief Justice had left for a luncheon engagement. As it was necessary for him to sign these papers, I asked the court attendant to take me to his house. But when we got there he had already left for the luncheon. The court attendant waited with the papers, had them signed and took them back to our lawyer, Dhankar. Tim left at once for Agra. But I had a lot of clearing up to do before I left, and the first order of business was to call the wire services to relay the news of our caravan's departure from Jaipur.

The Times of India – 25 October

Jaipur – The Rajasthan High Court today suspended the condition attached with a bailable arrest warrant issued by Ms Chandrakala Yadav, judicial magistrate, against Mr Ismail Merchant and Mr Tim Van Rellim, producer and co-producer respectively of the much publicized film *Deceivers*, and allowed them to leave Jaipur.

They will now proceed to Agra to attend shooting schedules there. The High Court has, however, directed them to be present in Jaipur on 28 October unless the regular bench of the High Court grants them an exemption on 27 October.

Both the producers were earlier directed by Ms Chandrakala Yadav, judicial magistrate, not to leave Jaipur till they appeared in her court on 28 October in a criminal defamation suit filed against them by Ms Sunaina Mishra on 19 October. Ms Yadav had even issued bailable arrest warrants against them and directed the police to raid Kamani House – the local office of the film unit – to seize any incriminating film material.

A police party, led by circle officer of the Ashok Nagar police station, Mr Rohit Mahjan, raided the Kamani House premises on the night of 21 October and seized some stills and papers relating to the film.

Mr Ismail Merchant, through his counsel, today submitted a petition before the acting chief justice of the Rajasthan High Court, Mr Justice Gumnan Mal Lodha, pleading that the lower court's order regarding their detention was wholly 'uncalled for and unreasonable'.

Mr Justice Lodha observed that 'in view of the extraordinary urgency and importance of the matter', the condition of their stay was suspended.

Whatever be the outcome of this legal battle one thing is certain, the pink city has not seen the last of this unsavoury episode. Even as the cricket fever would be over on 26 October after the crucial West Indies–England tie, the excitement for the Jaipurians would remain. Only the scene of action would shift to the High Court on 27 October and the judicial court no. 4 on 28 October.

But the one person who stands to lose millions in case the controversy takes an unseemly turn refuses to be cowed down. An unfazed Mr Ismail Merchant laughed off a question by this reporter this evening asking him whether the recent controversy would prevent him from making films in India in future.

'I will make ten more films in India and all of them will be shot, at least partly, in Jaipur. The Merchant Ivory Productions would stalk down the streets of Jaipur like a gloriously bedecked elephant,' he said.

On Sunday morning I went to Kamani House where all the trucks were loaded and ready to leave for Agra. Inside, that huge space which had been the centre of so much activity over the last six weeks was bare and deserted and silent. Everyone had left for Agra the previous day. Some of the people who had worked for us in Jaipur were hanging around hoping to come to work in Agra. But I felt they were all somehow connected with Bonnie Singh and I wanted to leave such problems behind. We had been allowed to leave Jaipur, but I knew the matter wasn't over. The court case had still to be heard. As far as the film was concerned, at least, I wanted to close the Jaipur chapter.

I also took the opportunity of this move to change certain things I didn't like. I changed the company from which we had been hiring our vehicles. They were overcharging us, so I myself arranged a deal with another company. Too much money had already been wasted. Because of our connections in India I could negotiate very good deals in matters of props, set construction, location fees and so forth, and in those areas our costs were well under budget. But in the matter of day-to-day affairs, transportation, accommodation and so on – all of which were Tony Waye's responsibility – there was by my standards far too much money wasted.

As is my practice, I wanted to settle the bills myself to make sure everything was accounted for properly. I also wanted to thank the dealers and the people who provided services for their cooperation. Of course we had paid these people for their goods and for their services but, as I have said many times before, money isn't everything, and I wanted to thank them personally and express my appreciation.

I had also arranged to take Bubbles and his wife around the set we built, from the ground up, of William and Sarah's 'bungalow'. They were so enchanted that they wanted to keep it as changing rooms for the club.

Finally I went to say goodbye to Begum Loharu and her husband Durru, a lovely couple who have an enormous house opposite the Governor of Jaipur's official residence. I had arranged for some of my team to stay with them, and they had also given a very enjoyable dinner-party for me, and I wanted to thank them for all their kindness during our time in Jaipur.

*   *   *

I arrived in Agra in the early hours of Monday morning after a
long drive from Jaipur and a flat tyre just one kilometre from
the Moghul Sheraton Hotel, where we were staying.

I remembered coming to an unspoiled Agra some twenty
years earlier with Shashi and Jennifer and Felicity Kendal. I
think we were looking for possible locations for *Shakespeare
Wallah*. We stayed at Laurie's Hotel, which was then run by
an English family. It was the best hotel in Agra, of the old
British raj sort – genteel, quiet, its nineteenth-century
standards impeccably maintained by a martinet memsahib.
This was before the days of international chain hotels setting
up their operations in India. Laurie's is still there but it's
shabby and run down, and the restaurant in the garden, where
we used to enjoy delicious meals, now only serves sandwiches
and occidental snacks. Mass tourism was bound to change the
character of Agra where the Taj Mahal, the monument to
love, is the principal attraction of the city. Built by the
Emperor Shah Jehan for his wife Mumtaz as her tomb, the Taj
Mahal is, for most people, the symbol of India.

On our earlier trip to Agra, Ken and I had seen three period
horse-drawn carriages which the Moghul Sheraton Hotel uses
for sightseeing trips around the city. We later negotiated the
use of the carriages for the wedding scene in *The Deceivers*,
which added to the production value of the film.

At the Agra Club, Ken had already erected the white
marquees in the club garden opposite a wide doric-columned
terrace that would be the principal set of the party scene.
Candles had been suspended from the ceiling in glass bell-jars
and the elaborate table decorations were being arranged and
rearranged by Ken and his team until the setting was
absolutely right. I liked the simplicity and the stylishness of
the set and the contrast it made to the extravagance of the
Indian interiors we had filmed in Jaipur and would be filming
in Khajuraho.

Nearly all of the credit for the film's 'look' must go to Ken Adam and Walter Lassally. They are both exceptionally fine artists, though sometimes they didn't get on very well together. It was the old struggle between the aspirations of the production designer clashing with the realities of a shooting schedule, of which the lighting cameraman bears the brunt. One might have supposed they would be natural allies, working as they did with a director who did not always have their priorities – the 'look' of the film – uppermost. It seemed curious to me, because they share similar backgrounds and have so much in common. They both are German refugees who went to England at an early age and into the movie business, and both are highly distinguished and acclaimed artists in their own fields.

The scenes in Agra required many European extras (even Michael White got into costume at this stage), and we began recruiting European and American visitors. We never have any difficulty in finding people to work as extras because most people are very excited by the idea of appearing in a film. It took several weeks of preparation to recruit the extras for this scene. I put Alex Rooks, a very resourceful young man, in charge of finding the extras – mostly from the various diplomatic corps in Delhi – and for arranging costume fittings and all the other complicated logistics when large numbers of people are involved in a period film.

The members of the Agra Club were very pleased about our shooting there as a large fee had been negotiated for its use; the secretary of the club was looking in a rather proprietary manner at a few pieces of furniture that had been designed for the set by Ken for Wilson's study, and the club's staff could look forward to the perks that always accompany the shooting of a film: tips and bonuses, and out-of-work nephews finding temporary jobs.

Halfway through shooting in Agra I had to go to Delhi to see the Ministry of Information and Broadcasting, and I had also been invited to give an interview on Indian television. As the programme was largely concerned with discussing the controversy surrounding *The Deceivers*, it was a valuable opportunity for me to put forward what I had to say about the matter. I found the tone of the programme and particularly that of Shashi Kumar, who was conducting the interview, enormously sympathetic. He also discussed and showed clips from our previous Indian films, which visibly demonstrated in the light of the accusations against us that Indian culture and Indian feelings had nothing to fear from me or *The Deceivers*.

I returned to Agra from Delhi by car with Tariq Yunus, who had just arrived back from London to finish the film. Tariq did not receive a very warm welcome from the unit, as the earlier episode still weighed heavily on the minds of Tim and some of the other production people. Tony Waye was the first person to greet Tariq in Agra; he told him that he had come back a day too early, that there was no accommodation for him and, most unwelcoming of all, it wouldn't be paid for if he did manage to find a place to stay.

Films take many months to prepare, but shooting always seems to come to an end very quickly. We were in Agra for less than a week, yet there was still a lot of clearing up to do before we left. The props that had been made, the tents and the awnings, were all sold to the Agra Club. The padre of the Cathedral where we had filmed had asked us to repaint it when we were finished and also requested that the front of his own private residence get a going over. This sort of thing cannot be avoided and, in this case, the precarious nature of what is left of the old Anglican or Episcopal Church in India (now called the Church of India) softened our hearts somewhat.

En route to the panchayat *– with a
lucky travelling companion*

Signing the agreement with the panchayat

At the school in Chandra Nagar

(Left) The Rajgarh Palace (Khajuraho, Madhya Pradesh), and (above) at the entrance to the Rajgarh Palace

Feringea (Tariq Yunus) and the thugs pray to Kali
(above)
Preparing an effigy of the goddess Kali (left)

(Above) *The thugs overtake a group of
travellers (Mausania, Madhya Pradesh)*

(Below) *Filming the ferry-crossing scene
(Chaukan, Madhya Pradesh)*

CHAPTER VIII
FACING TIGERS

The distance from Agra to Khajuraho is only 242 miles, but as far as accessibility is concerned, Khajuraho could be on the moon. There is no rail connection to the town: the nearest railway station is at Harpalpur, a three-hour drive from Khajuraho along difficult and sometimes dangerous roads. There is an airport, but flights to Khajuraho are few, erratic and always overbooked, particularly during the tourist season. The only certain way of getting everyone there was by chartering a plane.

Khajuraho has absolutely none of the essential facilities for the film-maker. It is so remote there are no telephones, no telex connections, no direct contact with the outside world, beyond the daily plane and that, too, is unreliable, as the flights are often cancelled. But for all its practical drawbacks, Khajuraho has every cinematic advantage. For us, the lush green landscape was exactly what we needed as a direct contrast to the parched crust of Rajasthan. It was cooler and wetter here, and the atmosphere was quite different. It had all the natural features and, above all, it had a wide river for our important ferry scene – or *The African Queen, Part II*, as someone called it.

Khajuraho was the religious capital of the Chandels, the dynasty that ruled over central India between the ninth and thirteenth centuries. It is a place of extraordinary beauty combined with great cultural interest, and is known to travellers and art lovers for the architecture and sculpture of the thousand-year-old temples, with their erotic reliefs of copulating couples in every imaginable position. The state of Madhya Pradesh is so far off the beaten track that when the harried visitor finally gets there and begins to look around and to get his bearings, he feels that he is at last in the 'real India' –

a timeless India of natural beauty, unspoilt villages and more benign weather. Wide rivers flow through peaceful landscapes in which forests of teak and feathery peepul trees cast a welcoming shade. There are wild beasts and also wild men about, but that only adds to the interest of the place.

We knew there were going to be tremendous problems with accommodation in Khajuraho. Even though we had made our arrangements many months before our arrival, we still couldn't get the number of rooms we needed because November is the height of the tourist season. So we not only had fewer rooms, but we also in some instances had to use a lower grade of hotel than the ones we had been using until now. Because of this room shortage, we had asked when still in Jaipur for volunteers who would be willing to share for an additional per-diem payment. There are only seven hotels in Khajuraho, and of those only two have the facilities film crews have come to expect. We accommodated as many people as we could in the two large hotels and split the rest between the smaller hotels which were not as comfortable.

The Indian crew were very cooperative and welcomed the idea of additional money. But a few of the English crew, led by Dena Vincent, the English production coordinator, Gerry Crampton, the stunt coordinator, and Alex Matcham, the accountant, refused to accept the reality of the situation and even persuaded some of the Indian crew and actors to demand separate rooms or more money for sharing.

Eleanor Chaudhuri, the Indian production coordinator, was trying to organize these additional rooms, and Tony Waye and Tim were trying to make satisfactory offers to the crew. A general meeting was called at the Chandela Hotel and I made a proposal – extra money for sharing rooms or else planes back home for those who refused. I felt that those who wanted to leave were not the kind of people I wanted to work with anyway. Some people took exception to my remarks and there were more meetings and more discussions. The bar of the hotel became the battleground. During all this fuss three famous bandits, just released from jail, came to the Chandela to meet me and ask for bit parts in the film. They were perfectly decent and seemed amazed at the sahibs' brouhaha, so I offered them drinks and tried to listen to their ideas for playing parts in the film as the discussions raged all about us.

I was very annoyed by this exhibition and Tim was equally outraged by these demands. I sympathized with the people who were expected to share, but there was nothing I could do and I felt that some of them were being unreasonable. I couldn't build another hotel overnight. In Jaipur and Agra, where luxury accommodation had been available, everyone had stayed in good hotels. But this was Khajuraho and they had to accept what it offered even if it meant having to rough it – not because I wouldn't put them up at the best hotels, but because these were the *only* hotels.

From the very beginning I had wanted to shoot this part of the film in Khajuraho, despite the complete absence of essential amenities. I was not prepared to sacrifice a unique location simply because it couldn't provide for everyone the four-star facilities film units like. In the end, everyone chose to stay. I had suspected that, as usual when things like this happen, it's a matter of one or two disgruntled people unsettling the rest.

When India met England in the semi-finals of the cricket World Cup, which was then taking place in India, only the Americans on the unit couldn't understand what all the excitement was about. But for the duration of that match it was very apparent that *The Deceivers* was not uppermost in the minds of either the Indian or the English crew. Shashi had taken charge of the radio and relayed the scores to everyone. He was so caught up in the excitement he announced that if India didn't win the match he personally would be dishonoured and would be forced to become sati. The Indians lost, but Shashi went off the idea.

Shashi has a bizarre sense of humour. For the scene in *The Deceivers* where the mass graves are discovered and the thugs' victims are dug up, the special-effects department had made hundreds of gruesome looking corpses in various stages of decomposition. As the skeletons and emaciated corpses were carried to the site just before shooting, Shashi looked at the procession and said mournfully, 'There go twenty-five years of Merchant Ivory actors.' I pointed out to Shashi that everyone complains of putting *on* weight during the making of our films, because of my interest in good food.

It has been a custom during the making of our films to have a weekly 'curry party', a tradition that started in New York when we were making *Savages* in 1972. I can't remember what we were using for money when we made that film, but at one point I sensed that spirits were low, so I cooked a lavish Indian banquet for the whole unit after the rushes were screened one Friday night. And ever since then my curry parties have become a feature of each film. Indeed, I have heard it said that my curry parties are sometimes considered an inducement to work on Merchant Ivory films. During *The Bostonians* Christopher Reeve went to the length of having T-shirts made up for the cast and crew saying, 'I did it for curry.'

Perhaps it was because we were coming to the end of the film and everyone knew we would soon be parting company, or perhaps there is just something in the air of Khajuraho, but while we were there the mood lightened and everyone began to be in a better humour, once the accommodation problem was resolved. On this picture, because of everything that was going on, I had had neither the time nor the inclination to prepare even one curry party. But in Khajuraho I did appropriate the kitchen of the Raja Café once or twice, where I cooked for a few of my friends. After one of these meals, Raffaele Vincente, the Italian prop master, announced that he, too, would take over the kitchen and cook spaghetti for me. I wasn't sure how Betty and Joy would feel about this invasion of cooks in their kitchen, but Raffaele wasn't a man you argued with. (Once, after a long day's shoot in Khajuraho, Raffaele had returned to his hotel tired and sweaty. On stepping out of the shower, he realized there wasn't a single towel in the bathroom. He stormed down to the lobby and, still dripping wet and stark naked, he demanded towels from the astonished and horrified receptionist. After that there was never a shortage of towels in Raffaele's bathroom.) On this occasion Raffaele excelled himself and produced a delicious Italian meal in the depths of the Indian jungle.

We were using the original courthouse in Nawgaon for the court scene in the film, and we had erected a gallows right outside the building. As I was standing there talking to Pierce he put the hangman's noose around my neck and we both began to laugh so loudly that people from the unit came to see what was going on, and began taking photographs. We heard Nick's voice shouting for quiet. When he came out and found that the disturbance on the set was being caused by the producer, he looked quite shocked. I'm the one who usually haunts the set urging people to be quiet and get on with the shooting. But this time it was I who nearly stopped the shooting.

After a week in Khajuraho I returned to Delhi. The question of *The Deceivers* was to be brought up in both Lower and Upper Houses of Parliament, and I wanted to be there.

The question was addressed first to the Lower House on 9 November. It was very brief. The Minister of Information and Broadcasting, Ajit Kumar Panja, was asked by the Communist Member of Parliament from West Bengal, Geeta Mukherjee, whether the Government had given clearance for the shooting of *The Deceivers*. Panja replied that it had. He was then asked whether the script of the film portrayed a distorted picture of Hindu culture, religion and mythology, and whether it glorified the tradition of sati and if so to give details. Panja replied that the script of the film contained nothing derogatory to Hindu beliefs and that there was nothing in the script which could be said to glorify sati. This answer satisfied the Member from West Bengal and she asked no further questions.

On 13 November the scene was repeated in the Upper House. Members of Parliament Gurudas Das Gupta and N.E. Balaram asked whether the Government had given clearance to *The Deceivers*. Again Panja replied that it had. He was asked whether the Government's attention had been drawn to the allegations that the film gave a wrong picture of Hindu culture and religion and was said to promote sati, and if so what was the Government's reaction. Panja replied: 'The Government is aware of certain allegations made about this film. The script, however, does not contain anything derogatory to the Hindu culture, religion and mythology. There is nothing in the script which glorifies the so-called tradition of sati.' With that, both Houses of Parliament, having been given the opportunity to discuss the issue if they wished, returned to more important matters.

I had had absolutely no doubt that that would be the reaction of Parliament. Parliament and its members have better things to do than debate spurious issues created by vested parties. It was a matter of courtesy for the minister concerned to reply to these questions raised by certain members. The questions themselves had been raised out of courtesy to some concerned constituents. What was most encouraging for us was that it was now widely believed that the objections raised by our opponents against *The Deceivers* had been motivated by self-interest rather than altruism. And that was to our advantage because, though feelings on suttee were still running high, most people objected to having a disgruntled, and to some extent discredited, special-interest group attempt to manipulate their genuine beliefs. Nevertheless, the criminal charges brought against us still stood.

The Economist – 7 November

... Mr Merchant and Mr Van Rellim have been formally accused of indulging in 'indecent portrayal which leads to immorality in public life' ... Some of the charges carry a two-year prison sentence.

Every politician from Rajasthan to Delhi has had to take a public stand on the film, usually against it. The film-makers say *The Deceivers* does nothing to glorify suttee. They point out that another film made in Rajasthan, *The Far Pavilions*, has a lengthy suttee scene.

In that movie local people cooperated with the film crew. The explanation for the change of heart, it seems, is that a prominent local businessman with political friends secured a good contract for *The Far Pavilions* but not for *The Deceivers*. Perhaps the affair is just another example of the difficulties of doing business in India.

Many of the rulers of the different states are related to each other by marriage or, more distantly, by earlier liaisons. There are very strong links between the Rajputs and the people of Madhya Pradesh, and obviously they have similar sympathies. Because of this, it occurred to me that someone might try to turn the people of Khajuraho against us by using damaging propaganda.

In addition, letters and telexes accusing us of being anti-Kali were being sent to prominent politicians in Bengal (where Kali is most venerated), in an attempt to secure the support of the Government of Bengal.

What annoyed me most about our opponents was that they were trying to persuade people that our film could have an effect on any of the real problems India faces. We would leave India and, whether or not we took our suttee scene with us, or never shot one at all, the real problems of suttee would remain. This issue would not be resolved one way or the other (or even affected) by a mocked-up suttee on a strip of celluloid. If they had really been so concerned about suttee there would have been more value, and perhaps more effect, in addressing the people of Rajasthan directly, of trying to re-educate them, in order to get them to relinquish what most Indians today hold are barbaric beliefs.

Furthermore, by objecting to, and trying to suppress, the story of thuggee, they were in effect censoring Indian history. Thuggee is not an attractive part of our history but it is as much a part as the raj, as Partition or the assassination of the two Gandhis. Thuggee is not mythology or legend: it is fact. There isn't a country in the world whose history is beyond reproach. And much of those dark and ugly pasts have been the source and inspiration of some of the greatest artistic expressions.

Friends and colleagues abroad were becoming quite disturbed by the reports they heard from India. Jim decided to come to India and offer his support. He arrived during the Parliamentary hearings, and we returned to Khajuraho together.

I had now become accustomed to the certainty that each time I left, new problems would materialize which I would have to face on my return. This time was no exception.

The unit had been shooting the scenes where the mass graves are discovered and the many, many corpses dug up. A rumour had spread amongst the townspeople that we were not a film unit at all but a team of Italian anthropologists and archaeologists, experts in buried treasure, and we had come to dig for gold. The *panchayat* was considering what to do about it.

The *panchayat* is a form of local self-government, very ancient in origin, dealing mostly in matters of justice within the community. It is composed of a group of five (*panch* is the Sanskrit word for five) village elders appointed by the local community as their representatives. Anything that affects the community comes within their jurisdiction. They have no official powers, but they manage somehow to control everything in the immediate area, and it's best not to antagonize them or incur their disapproval.

I soon discovered that was exactly what the unit had managed to do while I had been away.

The site near Raipur which we had selected for shooting the scene where the 'corpses' are discovered was near an old and disused temple. Our digging ground was not a part of the temple and permission to shoot there should have been given to us, but our location manager in Khajuraho, R.P. Sondhi, had not cleared it with the *panchayat* first. Moreover, I was told that Sondhi had underpaid some local labourers and inflated their receipts, including one for the use of a farmer's land. The *panchayat* took all this very seriously and warned Sondhi that we would not be allowed to shoot in the district; they would put up road-blocks to keep us out.

Jim and I were driving to Raipur for the night shoot, and as we approached the village of Chandra Nagar we noticed that there was a road-block and that all the MIP cars and trucks had been stopped and barred from proceeding to Raipur. Earlier in the day Tim had told me there had been some trouble because of the amount of traffic passing through the villages, and that he was sorting it out.

Jim got out of the car and went to talk to Walter and Nick, who were waiting with the rest of the crew by the side of the road. I went to see the *panchayat* to find out what was going on. Tim, Tony and Chris Carreras, the assistant director, were already there, sitting with the *panchayat* and looking very out of place, not understanding what was going on or what was being said. The *panchayat* seemed pleased to see me. Lokendra Singh was explaining our position, and he introduced me to the village elders. We spoke in Hindustani. It seemed superfluous to have Tim, Tony and Chris sitting and staring at the *panchayat* and I suggested that they leave. I then listened to the people's complaints against us. It had been said that we were desecrating the temple and, as if this were not bad enough, that we were taking advantage of local labourers. The local people who were providing goods and services to the film were being made to sign receipts for much greater amounts than they were receiving. In addition, one of the unit drivers had offered money to a local village girl in return for sexual favours. The three-part complaint had been lodged with the local authorites and the police superintendent by the *panchayat*. It was a serious charge and no minor problem, as had been suggested. In fact, the road-block was the first rally in a full-scale war they were about to wage on us. A few of the *panchayat* members were also retired dacoits. Anyone in Madhya Pradesh can carry a gun, and several of the men in the *panchayat* had rifles slung over their shoulders. It was a tense scene.

I found many of the allegations very disturbing, and I told the *panchayat* that I would do something about their complaints immediately. They asked me if I would be willing to donate something towards the local school which would help the children of the village. I felt sympathetic, and Lokendra and I decided to visit the school; we made an appointment with the *panchayat* to be taken there. We also wanted any contribution we made to have the blessing of the Collector of Chattarpur and we decided to visit him the following day.

When I left the *panchayat* I immediately went to find Sondhi, who had been responsible for issuing the false receipts, and also the driver who had propositioned the village girl. Tim approached me and said he would like to handle the dismissal of Sondhi, and I agreed. The driver was admonished and was given a warning. He pleaded innocence and I felt sorry for him. He *might* have propositioned the girl, or he might have tried to flirt with her and nothing more, or *she* might even have offered her services to him. Who knows? But

I made sure it was impressed on him that he must be on his guard and keep away from that kind of trouble from now on.

The following morning I received a message that the Collector wanted to see me urgently, so Lokendra and I drove to his house. An official complaint had been lodged with him by the *panchayat*, and if they decided to stop the shooting the matter would be out of his hands and there would be nothing he could do about it. The Government machinery could only move slowly to protect us. In these remote regions local issues were dealt with by local courts. He advised me to try and sort the problems out directly with the *panchayat* in a friendly manner, and not to involve the Collector or the Government, because that would antagonize the *panchayat*. He reminded me that this was dacoit land, and to watch my step.

I took Lokendra Singh with me for my second meeting with the *panchayat* on Sunday morning. As we began our drive a butterfly flew into the car and landed on my index finger. Lokendra told me not to move because a butterfly landing on one's finger is a sign of good luck. Although it was a long and bumpy ride the butterfly remained perched on my finger until we arrived at the meeting place. When the car stopped the butterfly flew away.

We entered the *panchayat* building and were greeted warmly by the elders. Lokendra Singh's feet were touched as a mark of respect; in India royalty still commands these gestures. We sat down with the *panchayat* and began to talk. The most respected member of the *panchayat* had been a dacoit who, it was rumoured, had killed thirty people – and he was on the negotiating team. We went to see the school: it was a small mud cottage. I agreed to donate Rs20,000, which would be done with the blessing of the Collector. I wanted to make it official and I also wanted to make certain the money went towards the school. The *panchayat* agreed to this and we were promised their full support for the rest of the filming.

They also promised to withdraw the charges and complaints that they had lodged with the police. Some of the villagers, who were also active dacoits, offered to serve as security guards on the film. I thought, well, these people may be dacoits but at least they're direct; they want money for their school and they're not feigning concern about Indian culture in order to get it.

That afternoon I went with Lokendra to the Rajgarh Palace, which now belonged to the Government of India, having been given to the state by the Maharaja of Chattarpur at the time of Partition in 1947.

The Rajgarh Palace was one of the chief reasons we were in Khajuraho. It is an imposing and stately building at the top of a hill, and its carved domes and turrets dominate the skyline. We had decided this would be the perfect setting for Chandra Singh's Durbar Hall, where he would hold court.

Ken and Letizia were already at work there. Rather than the strong, vivid colours that had been used for the other Indian sets, Ken had decided to use pastel shades for the durbar in order not to distract from the hall's elaborate architectural features. The Maharaja of Jaipur had lent us some dhurries and other pieces which seemed right for Chandra Singh's palace. The local craftsmen were constructing a huge birdcage out of bamboo for the central courtyard where one of the main scenes would be played.

I had a great many ideas about the best ways of exploiting the photogenic features of this palace and I discussed them with Ken, who was receptive and enthusiastic. I suggested certain props and some unusual hanging-lamps which are called *hundis* and are seen in old photographs and nineteenth-century miniature paintings of durbars. I knew I could find these things in Bombay.

I had another reason for going to Bombay. I wanted Jim to direct the tiger inserts of the hunt sequence, which we had originally planned to shoot after we had finished the film. As Jim was with us I thought it would be a good idea, and save time, to do it then. The tiger hunt is one of the most visually exciting and dramatically important scenes in the film; the native beaters spilling out of the brush, followed by a stately procession of elephants ridden by British officers in large, box-like howdahs. We had shot the scene in Jaipur, but we needed tiger close-ups to complete it as, obviously, we could not have had a real tiger running loose on the set. The close-up shots of a real tiger would be worked into the scenes of the tiger hunt we had already shot.

Jim now began to take considerable interest in the day-to-day shooting of the film and – to himself, I think – justify his presence on the set. He had seen quite a lot of the rushes in London and his reaction to them was extremely gratifying; he sent enthusiastic cables and messages like: 'Agra scenes of ball and wedding look superb. All departments are to be congratulated.'

Just before leaving for Bombay I was having a drink with Walter and Jim. In the lobby of the hotel I saw Major Chandra Kant with the head of the *panchayat*. I had met this local character in an earlier recce, through Betty and Joy. Kant approached me and told me that Tim had invited him to come to a meeting with him. I couldn't see any reason for Tim to have a meeting with Kant. To be sociable, I offered them tea. Kant told me that despite having settled our differences with the *panchayat*, our troubles were not yet over. I asked him what he meant. He replied that the dacoits, knowing about our shooting, were going to make trouble for us.

One of the reasons I had felt I could leave Khajuraho briefly was because I thought all our problems had been sorted out. I certainly didn't want to leave if there was more trouble brewing. I asked Kant what connection he had with the dacoits and just at that moment Tim appeared. The next moment I found myself having a three-way argument involving Kant, Tim and myself. Kant claimed that he had been offered a job on the film as our contact man in Khajuraho and Panna, instead of

Lokendra Singh, against whom there were some feelings of animosity and jealousy due to the fact he was a member of the royal family and had a great deal of local influence.

The man from the *panchayat*, who had been sitting quietly listening to all this, now spoke up to say that Kant had been trying to agitate the *panchayat* against the film. However, as far as the *panchayat* was concerned, we had agreed to donate money to the school and they were happy with that and there would be no problems for us from them. There was some kind of double game going on, and in the end Kant was routed, but this is an example of the murky kind of intrigues that bedevilled *The Deceivers* throughout.

For the first time in his life, Jim was to become a second-unit director. We had arranged to borrow a tiger from Bombay's Apollo Circus, where the animals are very well looked after. The owner, Jayendra, was bringing the tiger to a specially erected bamboo enclosure at Studio-Film City, a large studio complex miles from Bombay. Film City was built in a game preserve where tigers prowled around and the roars of the caged tigers brought out the wild ones; this scared the hell out of everyone. Ram Yedekar, Ken's Indian assistant, had come to Bombay some days ahead to dress the set as closely as possible to resemble the setting of the tiger hunt we had already shot in Jaipur. Nick had given notes to Jim with shot descriptions and also photographs of the original location so that the two sequences would mesh visually. This was not easy, because we discovered too late that the variety of tall grass which grows in Jaipur isn't available in Bombay, so we had to find a passable substitute. Jaipur stands in a desert and Bombay is on the shore of a tropical sea.

We had allowed three days for this shoot. Jim couldn't predict how long it would take; it entirely depended on the mood of the tiger, he said. At 6 a.m. on the first day we arrived at the studio where the beautiful beast awaited us as though

Feringea (Tariq Yunus) in action

Make-up artist Gordon Kay covers Manmohan
Krishna with blood before the Rajput is buried

The scene of the Rajput killing (Raipur, Madhya Pradesh)

Hanging around the courthouse scene (above)

(Right) *A scene for which the art department was not responsible (Chaukan, Madhya Pradesh)*

Special-effects artist Brian Smithies with the dummy for the suttee scene (left)

Neena Gupta as Gopal's widow (above)

The suttee

he were granting a royal audience. He was nine and a half feet long, very ferocious looking, and, confusingly, his name, like Ken's assistant, was also Ram. The tiger had a very unionized approach to his work. I was told that he worked best in the morning and that he also believed in working straight shifts. Eight-hour shifts – no more than that. I asked the trainer whether we could pay the tiger overtime after eight hours, but the trainer said 'no', that the tiger liked to work an eight-hour shift from six until two and that we would have to keep to that schedule. I took a good look at this creature, who lay in his cage lazily flicking his striped tail, and decided that it would not be a good idea to argue with him.

In the month of November it never rains in Bombay (though there were people that morning who said it *always* rains in Bombay in November), but it had rained the previous day and it was still very cloudy when we arrived. So we had to wait for the sun to appear, in order for the new footage to match what had been done in Jaipur, which had been blindingly sunny.

The atmosphere was very peaceful and not like a film set at all. We sat on folding chairs and ate bananas while the somewhat somnolent-looking tiger was put through his paces. He was a very smart cat. The trainer and beaters banged on the bars of his cage with sticks to force him to come out and, after two or three attempts, the tiger – like any actor – knew what he was to do: jump, run, snarl, etc., after which he returned to his cage until the next take. On that day we took four shots.

The next morning the weather was even worse. When we arrived at Film City it was rainy and miserable, and the only pleasing sight was the beautiful animal sitting there with a rather haughty expression, waiting for us. But like many great actors before him, his big moment was at the mercy of the elements, and he had to pace in his cage until the weather broke. Jim and I took a nap and so did the tiger. By mid-morning the sun appeared and we began the day's work

We had erected a rostrum inside the enclosure for the camera and the crew and the director – though Jim said he would be happier directing from outside the enclosure, as today the tiger would not be tethered. We were doing close-ups, so the thin wire around his neck which we could not see in the previous day's long shots had to be taken off. We were assured this was not dangerous if we kept our distance. The Indian cameraman Rajesh Joshi, huddled behind a grass-mat screen directly in the beast's eyeline, did not seem that convinced. The work proceeded: rehearsal, back to the cage, take, until we'd nearly finished what we'd planned to do by the end of the cat's daily shift.

Everything was going very smoothly, but just as we were coming to the end of the day, the tiger became temperamental. He was suddenly tearing around the enclosure, snarling and leaping, and then he headed straight towards us. I've never seen Jim move so fast in all his life – if only he shot his films as quickly! I was amazed by the agility with which he scrambled up the bamboo sides of the enclosure to relative safety. I stood watching and decided that if the tiger wanted to call it a day, then so did we. The ring of attendants banged metal buckets and waved pointed sticks to get the tiger's attention and they finally got him back into his cage. For one extraordinary moment I realized that he could have mauled or killed any of us, and that film-makers really do some bizarre and even dangerous things. But I would not have traded this beast, dangerous as he undoubtedly was, for the miserable de-fanged creatures they sometimes use in Indian films, which, moreover, have – horribly – had their empty mouths sewn shut.

From the first I had decided that Chandra Singh should have a pet leopard or a cheetah: sleek, alert, menacing – it was the final perfect touch for the scene in which Sarah comes, misguidedly, to the ruler's door for help. I also felt it would be a good reflection of Chandra Singh's character: smooth and graceful on the surface, but intrinsically malevolent. Both

Ken and Nick had agreed that this was a very good idea. In Bombay, Jayendra, the owner of the circus and of our tiger, told me that he had an exquisite cheetah and he was willing to bring it to Khajuraho for one day. I sent an urgent message to Ken and Tim to schedule the shooting of the durbar scene on Monday the 23rd, the day the cheetah would arrive. I arranged all the necessary permits with the police and the airlines for the transportation of the cheetah and Jayendra promised to construct a special cage and bring the animal to Khajuraho himself, together with three attendants.

It took us twenty-four hours to return to Khajuraho from Bombay. We took a sleeper train at 4.15 in the afternoon and arrived at Jhansi at noon the following day. We then had a four-hour drive to Khajuraho. I didn't mind the inconvenience of this trip, because I was in very high spirits. In the Bombay 'thieves' market' we had found exactly the right hanging-lamps for that scene, and the reason we took the long train journey was to take the boxes containing them with us, and thus make sure they arrived safely.

So I returned to Khajuraho in great good humour. I get very excited when I know I am making something look as good as it possibly can; when all the elements are absolutely right and working together. Every scene in this film should have its own magic and I felt that the durbar scene would enhance everything that had gone before and would come after. It was to be an Indian setpiece of the kind that I most like to do.

The first thing I wanted was to find Ken and show him all the wonderful things we had brought with us from Bombay on the long train journey. But before I could find him I met Helena Michell, who was returning from the set. She told me they had just finished shooting at the Rajgarh Palace and had completed the scene in the Durbar Hall. I froze. I asked her why that had been done and she said she didn't know, but she thought it was because Shashi was leaving and so they had to shoot the scene that very day. I knew that Shashi was not scheduled to leave until some time in the following week, so I thought perhaps something had happened and he had to leave earlier. Then Ken arrived looking broken-hearted. He was with Letizia, who looked grim. He told me that the shooting in the Durbar Hall had been done in a quick and haphazard way, and that my message telling the production team not to shoot until Monday had simply not been taken into account. Jim was upset and angry and for the first time had words with Tim. Jim described him as sounding exactly like those English waitresses who tell you in a satisfied tone of voice that something on the menu is 'off'; or museum attendants who tell you that a special collection you came specifically to see is closed to the public.

I went to find Shashi and asked him why he had to leave so suddenly, but he told me that he was going later in the week, as planned. Up to then I had been mainly disappointed, feeling there had to be a valid reason why the scene everyone knew we were so carefully preparing for had been shot. Now I was absolutely ready to murder whoever was responsible. I went to find Nick; as director of the film I held him responsible. But first I walked in to Tony and I exploded. I asked him why the hell the scene had been shot that day. He said, somewhat airily, that the director had decided to go ahead. I don't think I have ever been as angry as I was at that moment, and no doubt my language was appalling. I couldn't find Nick anywhere, so I left a note for him. Although I hadn't slept for more than thirty-six hours, I was too angry to sleep that night.

The next morning, still fuming but more in control, while I was having breakfast with Jim and Shashi, Nick came to face me. I think by that time I was more disappointed at the waste than angered by the cavalier attitude towards what I had been trying to do. I asked Nick why he had shot that scene the day before when I had specifically asked for it to be scheduled for Monday. I explained that I had made all the arrangements to bring the cheetah, that I had personally picked out props, all to make the scene look richer and grander, because the Durbar Hall was to have been pivotal in the movie. He apologized and said that Tim and Tony and Chris Carreras had told him that Shashi was leaving Khajuraho, but that apparently he had been misled.

However, there was something else he said: our message from Bombay that said we were bringing the needed *hundis* – the glass hanging-lanterns – must have been misunderstood. It had seemed we were bringing instead a number of *hundees* – which means IOUs in Hindustani. This was intriguing, Nick said, but he did not see why that should stop him from moving ahead in order to save a day in the schedule. What could one reply to that? Nick was clearly saddened to have lost this chance of enhancing the film, but the opportunity was gone and could not be recovered.

CHAPTER IX
IT'S A WRAP

T he original shooting schedule for *The Deceivers* had been drawn up months before, and our intention had always been to shoot the controversial suttee scene on the final day of filming in Khajuraho. There had never been any question of shooting that dreaded scene in Rajasthan. Had that been the original plan, then I think I would probably have changed it because, after all that had happened to us in Jaipur, there was the strongest possibility of provoking a riot on the set and in the town. I didn't think that the filming of the suttee would cause any protest in Madhya Pradesh but Jim was very cautious and suggested that we should abandon the idea of shooting it in India altogether and do it in England instead if, when the film was finally edited, it still appeared to be essential to the story.

We knew from newspaper reports that our opposition in Jaipur was still trying to stir up trouble. Mishra had attempted to mobilize women's organizations in Delhi and Calcutta to march and protest against suttee and by extension the making of *The Deceivers*, but she had found little support for this. She and her associates had also failed, in spite of their telegrams, their letters to the newspapers and the two court cases, to make any impression on the Central Government. Officials in the Ministry of Information and Broadcasting had indicated to me in New Delhi that they had no intention of submitting to Mishra's pressure under any circumstances, and had advised me that I should just continue to shoot the film.

Nick wanted to shoot the suttee scene before we left Khajuraho and I agreed with him. I saw the wisdom of Jim's proposal, but my own feeling was that we had to film the suttee in India. It would be costly to do in England, requiring some sort of studio set and the reassembling of the crew in addition to flying the actress, Neena Gupta, who played the widow, to England. However, Nick modified the original plan and instead of having hundreds of extras watching the sati, as they would have done in reality, he agreed to stage it with only the widow and a few relatives and villagers by her side. There was no great reason to have a lot of extras in the scene when there was an alternative, and equally effective, way of doing it. I admit that the original motive for this change was the practical consideration; it was a low-profile, discreet way of dealing with our problem. But it also struck me that it could be a very interesting and atmospheric way of dealing with a very emotional moment of the film. It would be the last image on the screen, and the widow seated alone amidst the flames would be dramatic and haunting. Would that be glorifying sati? Who can say? I felt not. In a film with hundreds of violent murders in it, would we be accused of glorifying murder? Would people who are against murder come forward later on and point an accusing finger at us? Would they be likely to, in a country where at least a dozen murders are reported in the newspapers every day? But wouldn't there be more point to that if they did, than to keep agitating about the supposed incitement to commit sati?

I hadn't wanted any crowds to gather for the last day's shoot. I wanted to keep it all as quiet as possible and just finish the scene and get out. So we planned it for a remote area far from any village. But, in the end, Nick had his extras; he had recruited all the Indian crew members, the caterers and anyone in the unit who could pass as Indian.

The pyre had been constructed by the river bank, and the suttee was shot across the river as well as closer up, through the flames. The shots were taken as the sun began to set behind the surrounding hills and the effect was starkly beautiful, if somewhat innocuous. The scene contained neither the horror nor the so-called glory of sati.

But I hadn't watched the sati being shot. Just as I had had

other things to do on the first day of shooting, so it was on the last. I had gone to Panna with Jim to thank and say goodbye to all the people who had helped us there.

My emotions at the end of every film are the same. A sense of victory, and a sense of thankfulness that it is done, and a feeling of sadness at saying goodbye to the new friends you make on every film. I have never made a film where I felt my belief in it had not been rewarded.

On 26 November, as the unit made their preparations to leave Khajuraho and India, I had one call left to make and one final obligation to fulfil. I went to Chandra Nagar for a meeting with the *panchayat*. In the centre of a small courtyard, a table had been put out with chairs all around. When I arrived the *sarpanch*, the headman of the village, greeted me in the traditional manner; he put a garland of flowers around my neck and I put another garland around his. The rest of the *panchayat* arrived and sat down with us. As I was the honoured guest, the distinction of sitting next to me was given to the oldest man in the village. Tea and biscuits were served. Some of the members who were dacoits joined us in the celebration and talked very animatedly about the murder that had taken place the night before in a neighbouring village – a feud between two rival groups. There was a small ceremony when I gave them the donation for the new wing of the school. The new building would be properly built and it would carry the inscription 'Donated by Michael White and Ismail Merchant. *The Deceivers.*'

We then went to the school, where the children sat on the floor and wrote on slates with bits of chalk. There were no books. I talked with the teachers and with the schoolchildren, who wanted to have their photographs taken. I stayed with them for quite a long time and, when I left, the *sarpanch* and all the village elders came to say goodbye. They told me that I would always be welcome in Chandra Nagar and that I was like a brother to them. I was very touched by that speech.

That evening, our last night in Khajuraho, I gave the traditional 'wrap' party for the cast and crew. Earlier in the evening I had invaded the kitchen of the Oberoi Hotel and, together with Helena Michell, who acted as my assistant, I prepared three of my own favourite dishes for the party. Specially imported wine was provided for us by a bootlegger from one of the foreign embassies in Delhi. The party was gatecrashed by some National Cadet Corps officers from Jhansi. They had consumed a great deal of wine and soon there was a huge row between them and Saeed. We had quite a time trying to separate them. Everyone on the crew became very sentimental, as they often do at 'wrap' parties, and attempts were made to forget old animosities and jealousies.

Tim's parting gesture to the crew was the following letter which went out, without my knowledge, to everyone who had worked on the film. The letters to the British crew had been duplicated on the stationery of a subsidiary company and MIP stationery was used for the letters to the Indians.

Dear ——

Re: *The Deceivers*

Now that we are practically at the end of our arduous schedule and are all due to go our separate ways, I would like to take this opportunity to personally thank you all for the hard work and endeavour you have undertaken on this production. I am aware and grateful to you in that you have sometimes worked long hours without extra recompense, and your support during our initial shooting week enabled this picture to be made.

I look forward, I hope, to having the pleasure of counting you as one of my crew in the future.

Yours sincerely,

Tim Van Rellim

This same letter went out to Walter, Ken and Jenny, whom I feel one simply could not address so patronizingly as 'crew'. These are the creative collaborators with the director on a film and should be dealt with in a more graceful way. We, too, wanted to thank everyone for their help on the film and I had already made arrangements. I had ordered from Delhi silver boxes to be engraved with both 'MIP – *The Deceivers*' and a *rumal*, the handkerchief the thugs used to strangle their victims. I gave the boxes to everyone individually with my thanks.

Jim came with me to the airport, where I said goodbye to everyone and thanked them for doing such a wonderful job. Arish Fyzee, the clapper loader, quoted aloud – with alterations – from Captain Meadows Taylor's book *Confessions of a Thug* to much applause.

I have heard, have read great tales of enormity about Merchant Ivory Production films, devised to make men wonder. But the events of the past two months transcend all fiction and previous experience.

On the following day, 28 November, Jim and I left for Delhi. I contacted Jagdeep Dhankar in Jaipur to find out what developments there had been in the case. He told me that a detention order had been issued by the court, forbidding me and Tim from leaving the country until 3 December. This news surprised me, but it didn't worry me. I hadn't planned on leaving before the 3rd anyway, because I still had business in India to complete. Dhankar explained that the judge was considering both sides of the case and also some new evidence in our defence. Although I didn't like having my liberty curtailed, or even the suggestion of it, I thought that to protest would not be a good idea, and that to challenge the order of the judge could only bring an unsympathetic attitude towards us.

On my last visit to Bombay I had put the issues of the case to my regular lawyer, Taher Doctor, for an opinion. Like Dhankar in Jaipur he felt the proceedings were not maintainable and the case would ultimately be dismissed. However, he did advise me to proceed with a case for malicious persecution and bring Mishra and party to the High Court in Bombay. I decided not to follow this advice; I had enough demands on my energy and time without adding to them by pursuing yet another court case.

By all accounts, there didn't seem to be any cause for concern, and Jim and I confidently made arrangements to leave for London on 4 December. But on Friday the 3rd I heard that the detention order had been extended by the judge and that Tim and I wouldn't be allowed to leave India until the 7th, after the case was heard. For the first time I felt that I wasn't *free*. I wasn't free to leave, I wasn't free to meet my obligations and commitments abroad, I wasn't free to do what I wanted to do. The previous detention order hadn't affected me because it hadn't interfered with my life in any way. Now I felt trapped. I hadn't committed any crime, yet the law must follow its own course and I couldn't challenge that. Rationally, I knew that it was only a matter of four more days and I would just have to stick it out, but at the same time I was apprehensive that the detention order might again be extended. The processes of the Indian legal system, which had seemed only a formality before, suddenly appeared far more hazardous.

I asked Jagdeep Dhankar to come to Delhi and meet with Dr L.M. Singhvi, a lawyer in the Supreme Court and one of the greatest advocates in India, and brief him on the case. In common with the other legal advice I had received, Dr Singhvi's opinion was that Mishra's case had no merit. Dr Singhvi suggested I should prepare an affadavit about how important it was for me to leave India because of my business commitments abroad, and if the judge in Rajasthan continued to impose the detention order I could then take the matter to the Indian Supreme Court, which sits in New Delhi.

Tim and I filed the affidavit with the Rajasthan Magistrate's Court. On 7 December Judge Farooq Hasan decided to suspend the detention order and we were free to leave. The case would continue in our absence and a judgement would be made within the next ten days. The considered opinion of all the lawyers who knew the case was that Mishra's petition would have to be dismissed by the court. These reassurances from Delhi, Jaipur and Bombay seemed to indicate that the end of this nightmare was in sight.

Jim left for London: there was no point in both of us waiting in India when there was so much to do in London and New York. I returned to Bombay and waited for the actual court order of my release, without which I could not leave India. It was due to arrive on the evening of 9 December, so I made arrangements to leave for London on the midnight flight.

The court order never arrived. It was being brought on a domestic flight from Jaipur, but the plane was delayed for two hours at Ahmedabad and was not due to arrive until 1 a.m. My own flight was leaving at 1.40 a.m. I decided to go to the airport – there would still be enough time between planes. I took my nephew Nayeem Hafzika with me and posted him at the domestic airport to collect the order, while I went to the international airport to check in.

At the airport I suddenly realized that in all the confusion I had left my passport and my ticket behind. I called home and a messenger was dispatched with the passport and ticket. Meanwhile, the Air India duty officer at the airport that night turned out to be an old college mate of mine, and he asked the Air India ticket clerk to accept my bags while we waited for the messenger with my documents.

There was no sign of the Ahmedabad flight: it never arrived.

When the last call was announced for the London flight I decided to take a risk. There was a court order for my release, so I wasn't leaving illegally, but I felt my heartbeat increase as I approached the immigration desk. I showed my passport to the immigration officer and he looked up at me. 'Well,' he said, 'you had quite a problem in Jaipur. We've all been following the case and it sounds very intriguing.' Oh God, I thought. If he's been following the case is he up-to-date on it, or does he think there's a detention order on me and I'm fleeing the country? But he went on, 'I've been reading that you are celebrating your company's twenty-fifth anniversary and I'm very happy for you.' And he just chatted with me for several minutes. Each time there was a pause I wondered if he would ask to see the court order. He never asked for it. He stamped my passport and I left Immigration for Customs. I had an irrational fear that I would still be stopped. I knew I was free to leave, but the piece of paper that declared me to be a free man was in the sky somewhere between Ahmedabad and Bombay. Until I sat on the aircraft I wasn't aware that I had been breathing for the last half hour.

While all this had been going on, Tim, equally under restraint, had passed through Immigration, too. He was not questioned either and he disappeared into the departure lounge.

By the time the Air India plane had reached cruising height my thoughts were already in London and on *Maurice*, which had opened well there the month before; and in New York and the lecture I would be giving on the 10th, and beyond that to the next film, which was to be *Slaves of New York*.

When something like this happens I don't dwell on it once it's over. I don't think about it. I just dismiss it completely from my thoughts. You have to think about other things. You have to move on to other things. You have to move on.

We have a saying in Urdu which has often been applied to

me and which, I suppose, sums up my whole philosophy: *Jise Allah rakhe use kaoon chakke.* Who can touch those whom God protects.

CHAPTER X
HEROES AND VILLAINS

At that point in the production of a film when the shooting comes to an end, there is a huge sigh of relief from everyone involved: a difficult mission has been accomplished. But that point is, in fact, only the beginning of the real film, the film the public will see, which takes shape in the editing room. In general, people are only aware of two stages of a film, the shooting itself and the final product they see in the cinema. Yet there is another stage, sandwiched between the two; post-production, which usually takes more than twice as long to complete as the shooting itself.

During this stage the director works closely with the film editor; sound effects are added to the scenes, dialogue is touched up, or shortened or otherwise changed. Performances can be made and performances can be marred. The best of the footage has to be exploited, the worst has to be got rid of. All this is a very painstaking, time-consuming and laborious process. One of the most important contributors now becomes the composer; the music he creates will heighten the atmosphere and the emotions of the film. Nick had chosen John Scott to compose the music for the film. He had been impressed by what he had heard of Richard Robbins' music, but he wanted a different sound. I know how versatile Richard is but I didn't want any more arguments, so I let Nick's decision stand.

Post-production is the dark area, where budgets can go skyrocketing if there is no control. During post-production for *The Deceivers* I was away from London, where the film was being edited, and I had to leave everything in the hands of Chris Brown, the post-production manager. In New York I received alarming estimates for 'mixing' the film several months hence. At the mix, or dub, or re-recording of a film, all the tracks containing dialogue, music and sound effects are mixed together in the recording studio on one track. This can go on for weeks and weeks – and on very big-budget films for months.

When the shooting of *The Deceivers* ended we were more or less on budget, but as our payments were made in England we became a victim of the Wall Street crash of 26 October 1987, when the sterling-to-dollar exchange rate became most unfavourable, and the interest rates for our borrowed money continued to climb.

I was worried and I felt it best to put my thoughts in a letter to Nick, warning him that unless we made some economies we would not be able to finish the picture and would have to shelve it until we could raise more money. When I returned to London I went to see Nick. Of course he had asked Tim to prepare figures which showed that we would be within the budget. I disagreed. One could easily see that the interest owed to the bank on a minimum of $4 million would come to $450,000 for a year. It was highly unlikely, unless the film was a blockbuster success, that we would have any chance of recovering this huge interest. If we had saved money during the shooting of the film, as I always try to do, instead of losing $500,000 through unnecessary expenditure early on, we would have been in better shape. One has to be philosophical about these things and move forward. We had to hope that the film would be so successful that we would recover this loss and be able to pay back the money we had borrowed. But how many films are that successful?

I had had meetings with Amir Malin and Leon Falk of Cinecom, who had been supportive all along, and they agreed to increase the advance for the United States and Canadian rights for an additional $300,000. Ernst Goldschmidt of Orion Pictures promised to consider an increase from the territories they control. I feel that if you have sympathetic partners in the distribution of the film you should be able to count on their support when there is a shortfall.

In order to assist the cash flow of *The Deceivers*, neither Michael White nor I drew our salaries. Normally a producer should get his salary in the same way that a director does; part during pre-production, part during shooting and the rest at the end of shooting. But this has never happened with me. As an independent producer I am always the last to be paid, and I usually have to wait for a year or two, or sometimes three, before I can pay myself.

I had seen very few rushes of the film, and at the end of January 1988 Jim and I flew from New York to London to see the first cut. I was very pleased with the way the film had taken shape, but there was some concern between Michael White, Leon Falk and myself about whether Nick was really getting the best out of the film footage – these are the traditional concerns and responses of producers and financiers who view a rough-cut. Nick, however, had a strong faith in what he and the editor, Richard Trevor, were doing, and we accepted his assurances. The film is, finally, the director's vision, and Nick had guided us thus far, so there was little reason to suppose he would not take the film on to achieve the success it deserved.

Back in India the repercussions of the political problems we had experienced were just as I had predicted. Three films – which began shooting after *The Deceivers* – shifted to south India because of the way we had been harassed in Rajasthan. And now the French film producer Phillipe Diaz is facing a similar controversy: objections have been raised over his film *La Nuit Bengali*, based on a book written over fifty years ago by the distinguished philosopher Mircea Eliad about the time he spent in Calcutta, and his love affair with an Indian girl. Permission had been granted by the Ministry of Information and Broadcasting for the shooting of this film, but women are now mobilizing in Bengal because the script is reported to depict a distorted view of Indian womanhood.

Our own problems were finally resolved on 24 February 1988, when Justice Farooq Hasan gave his judgement of our case in the Rajasthan High Court. Mishra's complaint was dismissed by the court just as all my lawyers had assured me it must be. I was naturally relieved and happy by the decision, but what gratified me most was that the judge exposed the case for what it was: a total sham that should never have found its way into the High Court.

From the judgement of Justice Farooq Hasan, Rajasthan High Court, 24th February 1988

... I have gone through the facts alleged in the complaint, and I find the complainant deliberately concealed the details of public interest litigation and also its decision, in her complaint. The complaint and the public interest litigation touches the same controversy in legal field as is apparent from the record, and the inference is precise and patently obvious because, the complainant has invoked criminal jurisdiction after the writ petition was dismissed. And, it appears that the complainant after having been frustrated by the decision of this Court in the hierarchy of writ court, has further enmeshed the petitioners in criminal prosecution which prima facie appears to be an abuse of the process of law. Day in and day out in courts petitions are accepted and rejected in favour of one of the parties. If in all such cases complaints under procedure codes are to be filed, not only will there will open up floodgates of litigation but it would unquestionably be an abuse of the process of the Court.

... After perusal of the entire record, it appears that Government of India has, while granting permissions, acted with utmost care and caution and has created adequate machinery by subjecting the petitioners to restrictions ...

Criminal prosecution in such a situation is glaring misuse of the process of the Court.

... I accordingly, allow this criminal misc. petition, set aside and quash the proceedings before the learned subordinate Magistrate, which have been initiated by him, being abuse of process of the Court and, therefore, the complaint in question deserves to be dismissed and thus the same is dismissed.

The petitioners are discharged. Their bail bonds stand cancelled.

In its way, *The Deceivers* proved to be another episode illustrating the long and sometimes strange tale of Englishmen and Indians together. If it demonstrates how the differences between the two produce discord, it also shows how much agreement is still possible. The film is done and everyone, I think, is proud to have worked on it.

But the role of the producer never ends. Even when postproduction is complete and the film is promoted and released, my links with it continue indefinitely. The financial problems of the film live on as I try to extract the money due from exhibitors and distributors around the world, which is just as much hard work as making the film itself – and sometimes equally creative!

But if film-making is madness, I am happy to be counted amongst the insane.

CAST
(in alphabetical order)

Ken Adam – Production designer
Letizia Adam – Wife of Ken Adam
Justice S.C. Agarwal – Judge in the High Court of Rajasthan
Mr Alhuvalia – Manager of the Raj Mahal Hotel, Jaipur
Naushad Ali – A friend of mine
Mikki Ansin – Stills photographer for *The Deceivers*
Colin Arthur – Make-up assistant for *The Deceivers*
Peggy Ashcroft – Actress
N.E. Balaram – Member of Parliament
Ben Barker – My assistant on *The Deceivers*
Jenny Beaven – Costume designer for *The Deceivers*
Kamla Beniwal – Minister of Culture, Rajasthan
Mr Bhatachariya – Editor of *The Times of India*, Jaipur
Mohamedali Bootwalla – A friend of mine
Paul Bradley – My associate at MIP's London office
John Bright – Costume designer for *The Deceivers*
Pierce Brosnan – Actor, William Savage in *The Deceivers*
Chris Brown – Post-production manager for *The Deceivers*
Chris Carreras – First assistant director for *The Deceivers*
Jenne Cassarotto – Agent for Stephen Frears
Eleanor Chaudhuri – Indian production coordinator for *The Deceivers*
Nirad Chaudhuri – Writer
Mr Chaudhury – Member of the National Council of the Janata Party
Mr P. Chidambaram – Minister of State for Home Affairs
Wahid Chowhan – My brother-in-law
Gerry Crampton – Stunt coordinator for *The Deceivers*
Gayatri Devi – Rajmata of Jaipur, stepmother to the Maharaja of Jaipur
Jagdeep Dhankar – My lawyer in Jaipur
Jean Diamond – Agent for Keith Michell
Phillipe Diaz – French film producer
Taher Doctor – My lawyer in Bombay
Leon Falk – Head of development, Cinecom
Stephen Frears – Potential director for *The Deceivers*
Franco Fumigalli – Art director for *The Deceivers*
Arish Fyzee – Clapper loader for *The Deceivers*

Ernst Goldschmidt – Head of Orion
Gurudas Das Gupta – Member of Parliament
Neena Gupta – Actress, Gopal's widow in *The Deceivers*
Nayeem Hafzika – Third assistant director for *The Deceivers*, my nephew
Justice Farooq Hasan – Judge at the High Court of Rajasthan
Michael Hirst – Screenplay writer for *The Deceivers*
Cyril Howard – Head of Pinewood Studios
Aamer Hussein – My friend and long-standing collaborator
Jeremy Irons – Actor
Jeremy Isaacs – Chief executive, Channel 4 Television, London
James Ivory – Film director and my partner
Jennifer Jaffrey – Casting director, second wife of Saeed Jaffrey
Madhur Jaffrey – Actress, first wife of Saeed Jaffrey
Saeed Jaffrey – Actor, Hussein in *The Deceivers*
Justice Pana Chand Jain – Judge in the High Court of Rajasthan
The Maharaja of Jaipur
Mr H.C. Jayal – Film facilities officer, Ministry of Information and
Broadcasting
Jayendra – Owner of the Apollo Circus, Bombay
Ruth Prawer Jhabvala – Writer and my partner
Harideo Joshi – Chief Minister of Rajasthan
Rajesh Joshi – Second-unit cameraman
Betty and Joy Judah – friends in Khajuraho
Bina Kak – Deputy Minister of Culture, Rajasthan
Marek Kanievska – Potential director for *The Deceivers*
Roop Kanwar – Widow who became suttee
Shashi Kapoor – Actor, Chandra Singh in *The Deceivers*
Kasliwal Brothers – Owners of the Gem Palace, Jaipur
His Excellency Pratap Kishen Kaul – Indian Ambassador to Washington
Gordon Kay – Make-up artist for *The Deceivers*
Felicity Kendal – Actress
Jennifer Kendal – Late wife of Shashi Kapoor
Amulya Ratan Kohli – Ex-member of the Ministry of Finance in Rajasthan
Government
Anthony Korner – My friend and collaborator
Manmohan Krishna – Actor, the Rajput in *The Deceivers*
Shashi Kumar – Television presenter in Delhi
Anna Kythreotis – Journalist
Walter Lassally – Cinematographer for *The Deceivers*

CAST

Justice Gumnam Lodha – Acting Chief Justice of the High Court of Rajasthan

Nawabzada Durru Loharu – My friend

Begum Fauzia Loharu – Wife of Durru Loharu

Amir Malin – President of Cinecom

Louis Malle – French film director

Rita Mangat – Travel agent for *The Deceivers*

Alex Matcham – Production accountant for *The Deceivers*

Mr Mathur – Chief Secretary of Rajasthan

Girish Mehra – Secretary of the Ministry of Information and Broadcasting, New Delhi

Nicholas Meyer – Director for *The Deceivers*

Helena Michell – Actress, Sarah in *The Deceivers*

Keith Michell – Actor, father of Helena Michell, Wilson in *The Deceivers*

Bhagwan Mirchandani – Liaison officer from the Ministry of Information and Broadcasting for *The Deceivers*

Govindji Mishra – Secretary of the Ministry of Culture in Rajasthan (no relation to Sunaina Mishra)

Sunaina Mishra – Social worker, friend of Bonnie Singh and leader of the opposition to the film

S.K. Misra – Secretary of the Ministry of Tourism, Central Government

Subrata Mitra – Cinematographer

Geeta Mukherjee – Communist Member of Parliament for West Bengal

Deepak Nayar – Indian production manager for *The Deceivers*

Sheesh Ram Ola – Minister of the Environment, Rajasthan

Dr Deepika Pandye – Unit doctor for *The Deceivers*

Dr Pankaj Pandya – Unit doctor for *The Deceivers*

Ajit Kumar Panja – Minister of Information and Broadcasting, New Delhi

S.P.S. Rathore – Deputy Inspector General of Police

Satyajit Ray – Film director

Vanessa Redgrave – Actress

Christopher Reeve – Actor

Joely Richardson – Actress, daughter of Vanessa Redgrave

David Robb – Actor, George Angelsmith in *The Deceivers*

Richard Robbins – My friend and long-standing collaborator with MIP

Eric Roberts – Actor

Alex Rooks – Unit manager

David Rose – Senior commissioning editor, Channel 4 Television, London

Fahad Samar – Son of my friend Kareem Samar

John Scott – Composer for *The Deceivers*
Bonnie Singh – Initiated the opposition to *The Deceivers*
Himmat Singh – Secretary of the Rajasthan Film Production Society
Lokendra Singh – Prince of Panna, contact man in Khajuraho for *The Deceivers* (no relation to Bonnie Singh)
Raghvendra Singh – Stand-in for Saeed Jaffrey on *The Deceivers*, brother-in-law of Bonnie Singh
Ranbir Singh – Chairman of Rajasthan Chapter of the Indian People's Theatre Association (no relation to Bonnie Singh)
Dr L.M. Singhvi – My lawyer in Delhi
Gilda Smith – Of Film Finances
Brian Smithies – Special-effects artist on *The Deceivers*
Colonel Sodhi – Commandant of the 61st Cavalry
R.P. Sondhi – Location manager in Khajuraho for *The Deceivers*
Shanmukha Srinivas – Young actor, Hira Lal in *The Deceivers*
Richard Trevor – Film editor for *The Deceivers*
Shahnaz Vahanvaty – My secretary in Bombay
Tim Van Rellim – Co-producer for *The Deceivers*
Ramswaroop Vijayvargiya – Antique dealer in Jaipur
Dena Vincent – Production coordinator for *The Deceivers*
Raffaele Vincente – Prop master for *The Deceivers*
Rajesh Vivek – Actor, Duleep Ram, the thugs' holy man, in *The Deceivers*
Basant Vyas – General Secretary of the Council for Social, Political and Economic Studies, friend of Bonnie Singh's and front man for the opposition to *The Deceivers*
Anthony Waye – Production supervisor for *The Deceivers*
Raquel Welch – Actress in *The Wild Party*
Natasha Wellesley – Daughter of Tim Van Rellim
Michael White – Executive producer for *The Deceivers*
Tony Williams – Head of production at Rank (1981)
Treat Williams – Actor
Roger Wingate – Investor, head of Curzon Film Distributors
Charles Wood – First screenplay writer for *The Deceivers*
Ram Yedekar – Indian art director on *The Deceivers*
Tariq Yunus – Actor, Feringea in *The Deceivers*
Balkishan Zutsie – Joint Secretary of the Ministry of Information and Broadcasting